THE MODERN ERA'S DILEMMA

JOURNEY FROM FALSE PROGRESS TO SPIRITUAL RETREAT

VIKRANT SINGH DADWAL

Copyright © Vikrant Singh Dadwal 2024
All Rights Reserved.

ISBN

Paperback 979-8-89544-540-2

Hardcase 979-8-89544-887-8

CONTENTS

Contents

PREFACE

When absorbed in thinking, an intriguing question or realization comes to haunt me and I am sure the same feeling might be haunting many others as well. What's this quest on which we are headed? What are we really chasing and in which direction are we progressing?

This feeling, realization, curosity and question, whatever you may call it, made me sit and delve deeper into this never ending thoughtprocess and write my own feelings, experiences, and observations. We are in the modern era of computers, smartphones, smartwatches and lot many more gadgets which have become an integral part of our lives. We call our today's state as a progressed state of humanity, as we have come a long way from where our ancestors *(the early man and the following generations)* started. But when answering this question of what are we really chasing? The feeling that's common is an anxiety that emerges and brings the realization that the chase is relentless and never-ending. No matter how much wealth and possessions have we created, the pursuit for more is still there and is growing continuously. So, it really becomes important to pause a bit, and reflect on this whole process of our evolution, transformation and transition from ealry life to modern world.

The whole journey of evolution is really fascinating with all the learnings around survival, discovery and progress. From the era of survival, we have moved into a modern era with survival and security being ensured, along with added luxuries and comforts of life. Despite our progress and achievements, there's a deeper introspection that's required and that's the question which keeps haunting us – "Have we really progressed?" The answer to this intriguing question is not very simple, as we can't ignore all the efforts being put-in to reach where we have reached today. But there are some important aspects and attributes of the "ways of life" which we missed on the way towards this progress.

This book is about the exploration of the journey that humanity as a whole has taken so far. Not only humans, but the whole planet has transformed itself over this entire period of transition. The book gets into all the different stages of growth and progress, the actions of humans, the outcomes and introspection. There are interesting but very important stories embedded from mythology that takes us on the journey of introspection. Reflections on the material growth and progress, the book uncovers the truth behind this growth and progress and answers – "what's achieved and is it really worth it?"

This book is not at all an intention to critize the growth and establishment of modern era, but it goes beyond the criticism and debate. It focuses on some really serious issues and topics that need immediate attention and action from all of the humanity. We need to work together towards the betterment of this planet, as this is what we have to live and survive and it's our responsibility to convert this planet into a heavenly abode. The abode and land of "God", to be passed on as a beautiful gift to the coming generations.

Readers are invited to join me on this exploration and be a participant and contributor in challenging the foundations of our modern society, uncover the real essence of – "what it takes to live a meaningful life?".

.......To the true seekers, for whom truth matters the most

.......Who dare to question the path taken and foundations of modern world

.......For all those, who still believe in living in harmony with nature

.......May this become an inspiration to think beyond the illusion, towards the wisdom and simplicity

"We are chasing our dreams, with promise of progress,

Working day and night, with an illusionary process,

The dreams we are building are like sand on the sea-shore,

Blinded to see the coming tides, our behaviours are of an immature,

We are seeking growth in the skies so high,

Hardly we see beneath, where the shadows lie,

There's still time to wait and hear nature's call,

True wisdom still lies deep inside us, waiting for us to fall,

Our path can become clear in harmony with nature,

It's time to accept spiritual retreat, love the environment and fellow creatures,

Embrace the peace and freedom of truth,

Wrap a beautiful gift for the coming generations and youth."

Chapter 1

THE UNENDING QUEST FOR HAPPINESS –
"HAS WE REALLY ACHIEVED IT?"

The world today is grappling with so many challenges in different shape and form. We are faced with food crisis, unemployment, wars, shelter crisis and the list go on. We say that we are heading towards the pinnacle of evolution and growth. This should ideally mean that we are getting better every single day as we progress, but sadly that's not the case. It appears as if we have forgotten the foundations with which we started our evolution, or we always wanted to evolve in this way only, where we have resistance between people, groups and communities. We say today that we are part of a global ecosystem and to support that we created so many fancy terms such as global economy, ecosystem etc., but the real problem is still not getting addressed. We are just looking at growth and that growth is very selfish in nature.

What's the definition of growth for us today? – this is the real question we need to ask ourselves. Is growth meaning selfishness, working for betterment of a group or community or country or region at the cost of controlling and exploiting others. If that's the definition then we have got it all wrong and we are making ourselves head towards a disaster. We were hit by a pandemic just a year or two ago *(in 2019)* and ideally as a good society we should have started looking at the well-being of people around the globe, but what happened was reverse. Everybody just started looking for opportunities and jumping on them for sake of fulfilling their selfish objectives. Having piles of currency lying in our locker or bank accounts is not going to serve any good to anyone. What's the use of that growth which will one day come to haunt us and that's happening.

What did we learn from the pandemic? There were many learnings which we got and the very first one was **"union"**. It's very important for a community to assemble and work together for betterment when faced with challenges and that was seen in pockets during pandemic. We rushed to develop a cure for everyone so that humanity could be saved. But parallelly, we also started exploiting each other as well on many different occasions. Our intentions shifted in a blink of eye and we saw ourselves trapped in the never-ending cycle of exploitation in the name of growth and economy. Markets never went silent, but instead money started flowing across boundaries so that it could be doubled, tripled and so on. Corporations shifted their working models to show support to their employees in the name of virtual working, digital etc. Those who were ready to exploit got the opportunity to do so and those who were trapped in this never-ending cycle were ready to be exploited. We got a very important learning that we are controlled by our selfish objectives and that's something to be worried about.

The world has become a place where everybody is busy doing something. World is so busy doing something that no one has got time to stop and think about the society as a whole. What are we trying to create here. What kind of world do we need to live in. Do we need a world where everyone is a prey to others or do we want a world where everyone is part of a common support system. It's high time that we start thinking about this, before we lose time to even think and do anything about it. Growth for corporations is fine as they are meant to be focused on growth, but we need to rethink our priorities that at what cost that growth is coming. If that cost is causing more harm than doing good then whatever we are doing need to stop and we need to look for other alternatives of growth. Economy is for survival of human beings and the society as a whole, but it looks like we have become such that we are making ourselves an engine of growth for economy. What's the use of such economy where humanity is kept as an option? Let's think about it and then look at our priorities that what we are creating and how far have we come in it.

We talk a lot about our success across the world. Everyone is very proud of the advancements we have made so far and our achievements in each and every sector. We have created so many sectors which are serving us and we should be proud of it. But we need to clearly lay down our objectives in all those sectors. Each sector is meant to serve some purpose and it should have an element of betterment for the society. If a society is getting impacted by any sector which is causing any kind of illness or affecting the health of people in one way or the other, then we need to rethink about that sector and its relevance and fitment in the whole ecosystem. Because if we don't do so then it means that we are not worried about the society and humanity anymore. But we are just worried about creating sectors just for sake of our own selfish satisfactions. Why do we need so many sectors, is a very important question to ask. But we hardly ask that question and we keep tagging along in each and every development which happens just for sake of getting a living. We should ask first that, "Is this even helping us create a life, or is it going to kill the whole life on this planet going forward?". If we start asking these questions, then on that very same day we would make ourselves headed onto the right path of growth and betterment for all.

We have some very critical problems in the world today and we just turn our back towards them and keep working on earning our living. But a day will come soon when there would be no life to live, leave **earning a living** aside. What would we do then? This is a very serious question to ask. But we would shy away from asking this question, why? because our selfishness has made us become blind to the real problems. We close the doors and windows and sit comfortably in an environment which we feel is safe enough for us and our dear ones to survive. But we never realize that whatever is happening around on the planet, is going to come and impact us one day.

This piece is in no way intended to spread any kind of fear and it's in no way written to challenge anyone, as it's not a problem of the writer or the reader, it's a problem of the whole world. The writer of this piece has been thinking for long about all this, observing the world around, to see what possibly are we trying to achieve. Today the writer decided to put it together to connect with others, who are really thinking about the planet and want to do something about it. There's a dire need for us to get together and start thinking about our real objectives, we want to achieve. What we want to achieve is very important to define, else it becomes a challenge to address what comes our way in form of development. We need a very serious introspection around our needs, wants and desires because that's where the whole story of humanity started from. What we needed? was all we started with, when we thought first about our evolution. We never looked back at, what we have become in this journey of evolution. Have we become more human or have we become just machines which we are creating every day to serve us.

In a way we have become machines and we have started surviving at any cost and it hardly matters to us that what's that cost we are paying for this survival. Human evolution has a very interesting story of collaboration, sensitivity and control. Our evolution was a result of loneliness, struggle and challenges. We started our journey with an objective to stay together to ease our lives and make a healthy ecosystem of life on this planet. But as we got together, we started seeing resistance among ourselves. We started competing with each other for the sake of differentiation and proving ourselves as superior to others. This competition further triggered the flames of division among the created ecosystem and communities came into existence. These communities too started having the competition and resistance between people and that gave rise to further division in communities and this division went on and on. Today we are in a world which is separated by regions, countries, boundaries, caste, class and so on. We call ourselves one humanity, but we need to think about it deeply that whether we really are. The answer would obviously startle us that we are no more one, but we have become so many that we are finding it difficult to live together as one on this planet. We have filled our hearts with hatred against each other, we are trying to control each other, we are planning against each other, we compete and want to become superior over others and that's the whole game of humanity in the modern world.

What's that which we need the most today? We have everything manufactured in factories, being provided to us by markets and consumed by us for our fulfilment and happiness. Our happiness is very limited today. We have started becoming the slaves of our own comfort. Look at the world around and see how we behave, how we live and how we are blinded towards things which don't belong to or bother us. We have slowly started becoming more insensitive to all the rest of world around us. We are becoming the prisoners of our own self. What's that one thing which is common between all of us today? If we introspect a little about this question, the answer would be – **"the search for happiness"**. We are searching for happiness and that happiness needs to be ever-lasting. We have always yearned for happiness and our whole journey is a testament of this desire. But in that search for happiness, we have become sadder and more discontented with our own very selves.

We wake up in the morning with a sense of heaviness and that's because we are tired of our endless chase which we are running every single day. Look at us in these modern times, what are we really doing with our lives. Are we really living a life. Before we answer this question, let's give ourself a chance to ask a very basic question that what this life is all about and why are we really born on this earth. To answer this, we would have to introspect a little bit inside and if we start thinking about it, we'll find that the life is intended to be a journey of pursuit, the pursuit of freedom, happiness and ultimate fulfilment. All these point towards a state which we often name as **"salvation"**. We are born to free ourselves from the bondages of this never-ending cycle of birth and death. But we never think about life in this way. But why is this the case, that's another important question to ask. The answer is that we are surrounded by this material world where we have those people who are relying and depending on each other, for things which are important for maintaining the comfortable and easy life. Everyone is dependent on every other person and in essence people need people to serve each other and, in that service, they are becoming much more bound to slavery and they easily accept the life they are living or they are forced to live.

Why we are so important to one-another on one hand and resist each other on the other hand. We are like this only; our evolution is a perfect example of our journey together. We invited each other to be together for the betterment and safety of each other, making each other's life easier to live and making survival of the whole humanity easier, but with collective living comes its own complications where resistance and control starts dominating and a few starts benefiting over the others. We need others for a reason and then we resist and compete with others for the same very reason. The reason is "selfishness". We are selfish beings and we are always trying to fulfil our objectives at all costs.

The whole humanity is paying the cost of this selfishness. We have made a whole world full of problems around us and the reason is our selfishness. We are still not stopping and we are continuously focused on making things that would make this world even a worse place to live in. We are depleting the important natural resources every single day and we are not at all worried about what we are creating. We are blind to our own intentions, as was Duryodhana in Mahabharata. If we go back to the Mahabharata story, we can clearly relate the situation with today's world where selfishness has taken over everything in humanity. We don't want to stop our so-called growth at any cost.

The purpose of life is a far-fetched idea for us today. Let's try and understand about the purpose of life from the times when existence started. If human evolution stories are to be believed then the humans are seen as in the state of continuous war with nature. We have always planned things that can provide us comfort, safety, security and longevity. We started with simplistic discoveries and then we transitioned to the path of scientific evolution where we invented many such things, which we cherish a lot and are proud of today. We have developed such complex systems that we can almost predict what's in store for us in this natural home in which we have created an artificial space for us which is very well in our control. Why we needed so much control and the simple reason is that we want security and safety and we want to design it in our own way. When humans started exploring the land for liveability, it happened multiple times that one group attacked and decimated other to take control of the land being inhabited. This continued for so many centuries and the same thing is still continuing today and if we try and understand the basic psychology behind this, we will arrive at conclusion that we want to control maximum we can. That self-centeredness is the weapon which is suicidal for us.

Evolution has its own due natural course and the same thing was happening with humans as well. But we wanted to control our progression so we chose the path of resistance and struggle. We rose against the nature and started out on a war where we dismantled the natural habitats to build our artificial one's. We are still in the state of resistance and struggle and this will continue, because the resistance and struggle always yield the same result. We have discovered so many laws and one of the important laws which applies here is that the more you resist, the more you will be resisted. We are resisting the nature and we are being shown multiple times that nature has its own due course and it keeps on taking corrective actions at intervals and we feel that nature is trying to suppress us. But it's actually the way of nature to tell us that the more you would struggle and resist my ways, the more you will increase your struggle for survival on this planet. We discovered and learnt that earth has gone through complete transformation multiple times and all these times there were different creatures who were completely wiped out and so the same story would be repeated with humans as well. But we consider ourselves as the superior beings who can actually change this course and predict the future events to prevent it. But we forget that nature always takes its own course no matter what.

So, the question comes – "Is this the only way of living, in which humans are living on this planet or there could have been a better way of living on this planet?". The simple answer is "Yes", there's a different way of living on this planet and that way of living is harmony. Living in harmony with nature is the easiest way of living on this planet. Nature has provided with almost everything that's required for the survival of any species which ever originated on its surface and the most important thing is that such things are available freely for consumption of everyone and even after everyone consumes it, there's sufficient left and more will eventually come in future for survival of the species. But we thought that things can be stored for tomorrow and we can secure ourselves by storing and hoarding more.

How are we living? This is a very important question to ask. This simple question doesn't require a very deep introspection or getting back into the evolution or human history. This could be answered by just looking at the way we are living. The day we are born we seek security and comfort. The very first thing which every human being is seeking is security. We need to understand this security before we move any further. As like any other living being, humans also wanted their survival to last longer and for that they wanted security from the harsh environmental conditions and deadly predators. So, the journey of having an artificial world within the natural habitat started and today we have created a living environment for us which is safe and secure. But let's ask that question again – **"Are we secure now? Do we have a greater sense of security sitting in the 21**st **century in the warmth of our homes?".** The answer might not be completely "Yes" and the simple reason is that our real challenge is not security, our real challenge is something else. What's that something else, we need to introspect that a little bit.

Let's dive deeper into this and start with some more questions. **"Why we need security?"** The answer is to survive, the next question is – **"Are we satisfied with just security?"** May be, not. Now we have more needs being originated in the name of security. We have shelter, food, clothes and much more, but still we need more. We need more for the future, for our future generations to come. We want to store it all together as we are very insecure now. So, actually what has happened is that we have become much more insecure than before, because we have become greedy. The greed for more has taken over security now. This greed has further pushed us to make this earth a living hell, as we want to store it all for us. We want to manufacture more, consume more, compare more and more and more. We are competing with each other; we want to control each other and take the share of others as well. We want more than what others have, because we are jealous, and we have given the name of competition to this feeling of jealousness. We have become more civilized as a society, but in reality, we have become more selfish with our evil intentions of greed, with underlying poison of jealousness in the name of competition, undesired actions to destroy nature in the name of consuming more and growing as a society.

"Are we happy?" When we set out on this journey, we wanted to be happy. But have we achieved that. May be, but we have become more anxious. The reason is the more happiness we pursue, the more sadness we accumulate. Because both happiness and sorrow go hand-in-hand. So, as intelligent beings we shouldn't be pursuing happiness in the first place and even if we are doing that, we should be well aware about the sorrows which might come and corner us. We are continuously producing more in the name of achieving happiness. But the more we produce and consume, the sense of emptiness grows internally. Let's try and understand this with an example. For an average person, the basic needs of food, shelter and clothes are important and that's something everyone works for. But as we start earning, we start accumulating things. Ever asked yourself – **"why we do so?"**. The simple reason is that we are in search for something which we name comfort and satisfaction. We start accumulating things for our satisfaction. But the more we accumulate material possessions, the more we become dissatisfied internally and we start seeking more. This becomes a never-ending vicious cycle and we die one day repeating our actions of greed throughout the lives. **"Do we really want this for us?"** I think, no. We can do a lot better as a connected society today, but we don't want to be one society. We just call ourselves globally harmonious world, but we have ongoing conflicts with people killing each other, trying to capture things that others own and much more.

Happiness is not the end-goal and it's not even a goal worth achieving. Instead, it's important that we should focus on living consciously. We are just living and there's no consciousness in our living patterns. We keep on doing things which others have told us or which society has been doing for so many years now. We never question the ongoing patterns and try to create new patterns. We just keep repeating the same process which is already set in this global society as part of achieving happiness without even knowing that this in turn will generate happiness or not. With so many generations being on the same path, we have learnt multiple times that these patterns will never yield different results. Now when we are discussing consciousness, we should first understand what's consciousness.

Consciousness is awareness and alertness about one's self. It's very important to understand self and its actions. When we start becoming self-aware, we realize that it's the most beautiful thing that can ever happen to us. Budha is the example of such life. Budha had every worldly possession at the time of his birth, his father was a king who can make the world around him as per his wish. But he didn't even think twice before leaving all those material possessions and moving out in search of something which is called awareness. When Budha moved out, he didn't know what he is looking for, as the trigger for him was learning about the miseries of life. He realized that with so many miseries in life, how and why this life is even worth living. So, this one trigger made him realize the truth that he needs to go in search for real meaning of life and living. We know what he realized and what he learnt. His teachings are pretty focused on self-awareness or consciousness. It took him years to learn about himself and become self-aware. But he gave those teachings to the world so that we can learn from those teachings. But the real challenge is living those teachings which is difficult. Having very simple methods to become aware are very helpful in learning the self-awareness. As an example, if we start focusing on our daily tasks and start doing all those tasks consciously, we will start seeing the difference. Our whole perspective might change around life and living.

All human emotions are good teachers for us. But the challenge is we hardly think in that direction and we just use these emotions as tools for creating more artificial life on this planet. We are using our energies in creating stuff that's perishable and we are not doing anything really meaningful with our emotions. Let's try and understand this. Human emotions of greed, fear, love and compassion help us connect with each other. We are connected as humans, as one society, because we all have similar emotional patterns and thus, we can live together with all these emotions working as bridges between us. If we love someone, then we take the opportunity of controlling them as well. The control brings in resistance and thus resistance create opposite feeling or emotion which is hate. Similarly, greed gives rise to fear. Because the more greed we have, the more fearful we become, as we become very particular about material possessions and we don't want to lose them. Thus, the fear of losing them take over. So, this reflects the problems which these emotions can bring into our lives, but how can we use these emotions beautifully so that we can make this earth a heavenly abode for all lives. The only thing to avoid when trying this is removing the self-centeredness that we have inside us. Just being selfless is the first step to use these emotions in a positive way. When we see a beautiful flower, it really gives us a feeling of peace and tranquillity. But do we go and pluck that flower to make it our possession, the answer is no, because as soon as we pluck it, it will lose all its further growth and will become lifeless in minutes. The essence is that nature has given us everything and that's for our use and to make us comfortable in our stay on this planet. But when we start becoming possessive about things and natural resources, we actually do more harm not to nature but to us as well.

So, the very first thing to think about and get rid of is the "self-centeredness". We need to become selfless if we really want to be nourished and want our generations to come to live peacefully with all the resources on this earth. We have already done enough damage and we are doing it at a very accelerated pace which means if we continue, we will be making our coming generations vulnerable to more natural calamities and pandemics as we just faced. Our ego, possessiveness and selfishness has really caused us a price and we are blinded enough not to see all that, which means we are blinded towards all of it.

World has become more digital today. We started with industrialization centuries ago. In the beginning, humanity lived in harmony with nature. We humans used to derive our sustenance from the mother nature. But, as soon as the winds of evolution started rising, our curiosity and ambition triggered the industrial revolution. With industries, we wanted to achieve more and for that more we created more industries and this led to more production. Now the next step was to increase consumption of this production and this led to increased consumption and so on. Humans have always wanted more to increase the level of their comfort and make lives easier, but they forgot one thing that with every single comfort being added to their life, there's an added level of stress and anxiety which took toll on their lives. We can say that modern man is living the most comfortable life on this planet. There are comfortable homes to live, weather proof homes, big buildings, luxurious hotels, big roads, super high connectivity with smartphones, provision to stay connected with the world at the click of a button. We have attained much, of what required much effort in the times when our evolution started. But when we look at ourselves today and ask this question to ourself – Are we really happy, peaceful and content with all this we have developed around us. There are lot of surveys being conducted today to answer that question and there's no need to go there to find an answer to this question. We have the answer deep inside us and the answer is we are not at all happy, we are not peaceful and we are very discontent with the life we have around us today. With evolution, we forgot the real meaning of evolution and we got onto other pursuits and those pursuits were not of finding answers to some basic needs, but to fulfil the selfish desires of some of us who really wanted to control everyone else and want to become the lords of the humans.

Happiness has no relation to material possession one has, and it has no relation to the achievements as well. We talk about our achievements today and while we do so, we have some hidden anxiety watching us continuously and we don't want to talk about it. Because if we talk about it then we will have to hold ourselves responsible for the destruction and the whole story of this evolution and we don't want that to happen. Humans has a very interesting trait and that's something which control us, that's our "Ego". The art of having self-proclaimed positions be it internal or external. When we do something, we talk a lot about our achievements and we never hesitate to add more to it for exaggerating it further. We are very fond of singing our own praises and that's something which really eats a lot of our energy. This single trait has led us so far and we'll continue till we are either wiped out from the surface of this planet or we see many disasters coming our way due to our ongoing deeds.

Ego has a direct relation with selfishness. The more ego we have, the more selfish we become. With this kind of approach, we continue doing things which we feel right and we never bother to discuss, get a consensus around it, instead we continue with the things we feel right. This approach has led to origin of many groups, sects, states, regions and countries and much more. We are divided by our ego's and we will remain so. Within these individual groups as well, we are divided and that division is the main parameter of our growth. This is what the narrative is. With this narrative, we are being controlled by those who understand this trait well and who knows that along with ego having a sense of belongingness and attachment is important. So, stories are being created for a common group to align them all under one group and that entire group is led with similar intentions. People hardly question anything when they are a part of a group.

Now a very important question arises here, why people don't question when they are a part of group. Why the common deed becomes the prime thing and rest all is secondary. Humans have always been afraid of staying alone. There's a continuous sense of insecurity inside us, that sense of insecurity always leads us to be part of some group, community or whatever we call it today. The insecurity inside us always guides us to attach ourself to some sect, group or even search for another person. There's a very interesting fact here to understand that we always want to choose the group or partner or community which has very similar kind of attitude, behaviour and thinking as of ours, as that's where we feel most comfortable. The groups with least conflict have the leaders where most corruption happens and the groups with most conflict are the places which are much healthier. The reason is that followers tend to turn a blind eye to anything and everything most of the times and this leads to people leading such groups take away most of the benefits for themselves and keep others on their mercy. **"Who are followers?"** We are those followers who turn the blind eye to everything when we become part of a group. We stop questioning the intentions and we stop thinking as well. Humans have this tendency of thinking and questioning less and following more. This is not something new, but it's what we are born with. With desperation of evolution and getting into a comfortable life being the prime dream of ours, we have come a long way into an era where we are thinking that we are comfortable now, but deep inside we have developed more insecurities. With these insecurities, we should be questioning more, but why we have stopped questioning at all. Let's think about this before we move ahead in this journey of understanding. We have developed a life around us which is more artificial and less natural today. We are living in homes that need ongoing maintenance which creates anxiety and stress in our lives, but we still want to make our homes more luxurious through more artificial accumulations and then we continue maintaining them. For all this accumulation and maintenance, we need money and that money needs to be created at the cost of our time which we keep selling to each other and live the life of denial.

We have already reached a point where we want more, but we don't know what exactly is the definition of that more. We have explored, discovered and created many things on this planet and if we look closely at all our creations, it won't be a surprise to arrive at a conclusion that all these things are mere replica of what nature has already provided us. There's nothing new which has ever been discovered and created by us thus far in the journey of our evolution. Let's understand this with some examples. We started with the very basics when we began our journey of evolution and the basics were – food, shelter and clothes. Nature provided us with variety of foods, vegetation, medicine and much more in form of all the forests that exist on earth. Natural habitats were always there, which gave us cues to create what we call our homes today. When the journey started progressing beyond the basics, we marked wheel as the invention, but in reality, wheel was discovered through all the circular objects that existed in nature and we took inspiration and refined these existing objects further to create something for our own use. Similarly, any invention we see today actually is a discovery by observing what already existed in the nature. But, as mentioned earlier that we have our ego that tells that we have done and achieved a lot that never existed on this planet. That ego is our biggest enemy.

Chapter 2

THE STORY OF DESPERATION, DESIRE AND MISERY – "THERE'S NO END GOAL"

Time and again, it has been proven that the pursuits of humans have been unsuccessful. What they always pursued was filled with their own selfish intentions, where others were involved just as part of achieving an end-objective. The end-objective was set by someone else and that someone else just used everyone by providing them with their basic needs. Basic needs like food and shelter for protection from the severities and dangers of predators in the open, were among few which every living being always want. Humans learnt the **"art of exploitation"** from the very beginning where some who were really powerful either physically or mentally started taking advantage of others, who appeared weak in comparison. But how did it all started, let's delve into that. Let's get a glimpse of the **"hunter-gatherers"** era and try to understand from where all of this started.

In the ancient days, when humans used to live as hunter-gatherers, there were few among the group/tribe who were really skilled at the art and they were pretty different from the others. Life was very tough for everyone as the dangers of open and predators was always there. These small groups used to hunt and gather food for their survival and they ensured that they stay together for their survival. But as the groups expanded in numbers, things started to shape up very differently. Some members of the groups started becoming greedy, as they wanted more than others. They were always in search of opportunity where they can get more food, better shelters and a special care and treatment. Slowly this trend started picking up across the group and within the larger groups, there started this emergence of small sub-groups of differentiated individuals who started bossing others around and taking more than their fair share. There were few who didn't like it and they started noticing it.

There were incidents that really stuck these few who started noticing and these incidents reflected the corruption that started emerging in the group/tribe. Few who thought them as superior or powerful over others started giving all their work to those who didn't complain and simply obliged. While others were doing their share of work, these selfish bossy individuals started taking the rewards for themselves, they took the share of others food, created special shelters for them and had special treatment as well. Those who were noticing all this wanted to raise their voice, but they also noticed that there was a pattern which has already been established among the followers *(those who were willing to oblige to the orders of few)*, as they were ready to follow those who can offer them the minimum for survival. Tough times made the situation even worse, as those who already attained the position of power were able to control the resources and their distribution. With minimum supplies, the followers were easily exploited and they weren't having any choice to deny and thus their only option was to go along with the exploitation. This also developed a general consensus and a common psychology among the followers that they were the obedient ones and they should be following the orders of those who are in position of control and power. They started to feel being protected by these people whom they would obey and follow along.

The whole situation didn't stop there and it was followed by a pattern of exploitation and inequality. The strong ones having control and power became stronger and the weak ones suffered and struggled to even meet their basic needs. The intent was never this when it all started, but it ultimately led to the situation where it was about struggle for survival. People started getting into groups and these groups differentiated themselves based on their access to power and control. The one's closer to the class of influence became their advisors and immediate followers and they got better access to resources and share of power as well. Then there were other classes below them who worked for them and they got their basics covered just enough to survive and so on. So, if we look at the situation closely, we can clearly see that the intention was just to stay together and survive in the nature, but the same intent led to classification, groupism, corruption, control, power struggle, polarisation and so on. **"Why all this happened in the first place?"** Let's think about it and try to understand this through a relatable situation in our day-to-day life.

To survive, what we need is just basics – food, shelter and clothes. When we get our basics in place, then what's the next immediate thing that comes into our mind. We seek security to get rid of struggle for basics. The need for this security arises from our insecurities and uncertainties about the future. When we got some time to think, we started thinking about our security, creating security for the future. We started to think more about the future and stopped living in the present. This created the need for accumulation and creating things that can make us feel more secure. But not everybody was thinking in the same manner, but few who started thinking in that direction actually led others to move along and be the part of the group/society/tribe or whatever we call it. So, a very important lesson here is that we need security and we care a lot about it. Even in the modern world, we keep on struggling not only for the survival but for securing our future and the future of our near and dear ones. But do we really need to think so hard today is a valid question to ask, when we have already achieved so much.

Let's delve a little bit more into security and understand that what have we really achieved in terms of security today. **"Where we are in this pursuit for security?"**. When we reflect on the journey of humankind, we glance through the stories of kingdoms, struggles between the kingdoms for power and control, people losing their lives and their material possessions in these struggles and wars.

Some kingdoms emerging as winners and some becoming losers and this has continued as an endless pursuit of power and control over what? – over the people, material possessions, resources and land. But in this whole struggle, what humans has achieved and the answer is – **nothing**. As today that security is still missing. No one knows when there would be another war or destruction due to man-made disasters and people would be losing whatever they have achieved so far as per definition. So, then why this whole struggle without any definite achievable objective. This takes us to another important aspect and that is **"security is not the only thing we were pursuing from the beginning"**, there's something else as well. What else we were actually pursuing and when we think closely and observe our struggles, we can see that we wanted happiness and fulfilment for something and that something is **"achievement"**.

As humans, we have desires and the desires have been continuously growing since the time we started the journey of evolution and it will continue till we humans continue to exist on this planet. Our basic pursuit of survival has created this desire of endless chase which we have been doing since our existence happened on this earth. The beginnings, as we have heard about the early humans, were very harsh and the environments of survival were very harsh, so continued struggle for survival was not a choice, but it was the necessity. Common goal for survival generated the need for forming communities and among these communities the resources were being shared which helped some with easy survival and some still struggled, as we discussed above as well. The basic desire for survival actually transformed into the **"thirst for power"**. What started as a natural journey of survival, a collaborative approach for co-existence actually got transformed into an insatiable desire to control and dominate. The ones who got into the position of power started manipulating the systems to maintain their dominance, leading to corruption and inequality. The real need for security actually triggered this cycle of endless corruption.

When societies were formed, the cycle of misery followed as there were those who oppressed and then those who got oppressed.

From the lords to colonial empires, history has many such examples highlighting the relentless struggle humans faced and are continuing to face. When desires go unfulfilled, desperation emerges and that's what leads to the misery for many. In the modern world, this endless chase and struggle for material wealth and power continues. The modern world has even more hunger for these desires which continue to generate more desires in form of new goals. As a goal is achieved, many new goals follows and this cycle continues endlessly. Many philosophers and thinkers have separated themselves from this pursuit and chase. They delved deeper into understanding this whole phenomenon and what they have written in most texts tells us that it's important for humans to enjoy the journey rather than remaining too focused on the goals or desires. But how much of it is really true, is a bigger question to ask. Let's go back to where we actually started. We started from the instincts of survival, moved to desires and then towards fulfilment, comfort, happiness and more. But if all of a sudden, humans start accepting the journey, would all this which has been achieved so far would have been possible. Some might argue that this would not have been possible, but I would like to present a very different view here. If satisfaction would have followed the "need for survival" and instead of focusing too much on security and pursuit of comfort and luxury, humans would have focused on mutual survival and survival of everyone, the world would have been a very different place today, but the irony is that the thinking hasn't changed much as of today and it won't either in the near future, as this cycle of endless desires will continue to exist.

Let's delve a little bit deeper to build this understanding further. Let's go back to the hunter-gather societies. They were the people who depended on each other for survival, as the harsh and dangerous environments then created that need and this was not a choice but rather a necessity for them. So, they started depending on each other for protection and started sharing resources that actually created some level of comfort for everyone in the group. The togetherness actually ensured multi-fold benefits for them along with survival. This put out the foundation of early human societies. But this little comfort when exploited got transferred as some viral disease when the size of groups became larger and then transformed into bigger societies. The foundation was right, but how that foundation got corrupted is the real question and the answer is **"intensions of few"**. These intentions of few who really wanted to control and get more comfort for themselves and for those who were their real favourites actually triggered the endless cycle of exploitation, control and corruption. We can consider these early symptoms as the seeds of exploitation and corruption which were meant to prosper with growing size of human race and that soon followed when societies grew in size.

The **"corruption"** was like an early sign of a disease which started holding humans as its prisoners. The disease was viral and its spread was limitless as we see with most viruses that emerge as pandemic and endemics in modern world as well. As societies grew in size, it also grew in complexities and complex hierarchies and structures started emerging. With more complex societies, a concept that originated was the **"accumulation of surplus"**. This accumulation of surplus started becoming the foundation of social hierarchies. Let's try and understand this with an example. When humans first discovered agriculture, they were able to produce more food than was actually needed. This surplus gave rise to another important transition in the society which created more layers and structures in form of new roles. Those who were able to produce more, were able to stop farming and take other roles such as leaders, lords or warriors. But this change and emergence of new roles also gave rise to an inequality. There were few who actually were not the part of survival struggle. They were free to do some other things which were less laborious and comforting. So, looking at them others also started aspiring similar positions and this led to a difference being created between the two classes. The class or hierarchy or group, all these terms started emerging in the societies and people started taking roles as per the need or their position in the ladder of struggle.

What we can clearly see here is a **"ladder of struggle"**. A ladder where the initial few steps are for the foundation work, followed by the next few steps for those who manage or control the foundational work and the next few for those who have the luxury of controlling the surplus being produced at the foundational level. This ladder of struggle clearly highlights the inequalities of the societies, with some people really becoming wealthier through controlling the surplus produce, wealth etc. and some still struggling to meet the basics. The struggle for power triggered with powerful controlling the resources and powerless toiling day and night to just make the basics possible for their closed groups or families. This is how the whole process of transition started and the new era of rulers took over. Those who controlled the surplus became the rulers and those who toiled became the labourers. The class formation started and then it never stopped as more classes and groups began emerging within the larger class or group. Lands and resources were being controlled by the rulers and those who believed in that ruler followed him either in form of their managers, ministers or workers and rest began to put all the labour for them.

There are many examples in the history where rulers showed their power through creating symbols of their rule and power and they did so to ensure that their legacy follows and the people can connect with the foundation with which this whole class thing started. So, when we looked closely its evident that need for security was the initiator, desire for comfort, luxury and control were the triggers of corruption. We can put it in a very different perspective as well where we can say that the need for security actually transformed into the thirst for power and it resulted in inequality in the society or group or tribe. The transformation that led to the whole new modern world is a perfect example of "what happens when desires are unfulfilled?". The desires that remain unfulfilled often give rise to desperation and the whole concept of modern world and various discoveries and revolutions emerged from this desperation. What was the real need and desperation, let's understand it with some examples.

As the societies expanded with growth in population, there was need for more resources, produce and other usable items for everyone. But the methods of production were such that producing more would mean more labour and more labour would mean more people should come and join the workforce to meet the needs of growing population. But then, it would be difficult for those who were hoarding the surplus and dictating their terms to provide for everyone and still keep enough surplus for them. Thus, the desperation and necessity resulted in industrial revolution which began in the 18th century. **"What was the real desperation that led to the transition?"** The societies started feeling the pressing need for efficiency and mass production to serve the needs of growing population and this need triggered a series of transformative changes, that resulted in a significant change fundamentally altering the human society. This transition was not easy for humans, as it came up with its own set of challenges, making the life more difficult for many. Let's try and understand this further through some deep-dive.

Before the onset of industrial revolution, the economies were primarily agrarian, and most people were living in the rural areas in smaller groups, working in farms or having small-scale trades for producing goods of need. The whole process of production was very labour intensive, as goods were being created by hand. This worked for many centuries, but with the dawn of 18th century, the complexity and struggle became much more intense and it became clear that this is not sustainable with the growing population and expanding markets. By the time, concept of global economy also started taking shape. So, the real key factors that triggered this change and necessitated the industrialization were population growth, urbanization and competition across different markets in the whole global economy. Europe, saw a significant population increase in the 18th century and this intensified the demand for food, clothing and other goods. As the agricultural produce improved due to innovations such as crop rotation, selective breeding, there was need of few people to work on the farms. So, the extra labour which was freed from the farms was available for working in the cities that became the new hub of growth with most industries being established there. European nations were competing with each other for economic dominance thus requiring to produce goods more efficiently to maintain the competitive edge in the global trade.

Industrial evolution was just the starting point of transition and transformation for the societies and the whole global economy. The increasing pressures of growth, need to produce more and address the growing need for more comfort and luxuries of controlling classes led to the new technological innovations that further helped the industrial revolution. Some of the key inventions that really led the transformation included – Steam engine: - That allowed the mechanized production and the development of factories; powered machinery, locomotives and ships reducing the time and cost of transportation and manufacturing, similarly other technological innovations across textile industry, iron and steel industry created the lasting impact on the society. The technological innovations helped with significant economic growth and increased productivity, but also had some really deep consequences. In essence, the shift from the agrarian economies to industrialized cities altered each and every aspect of daily life.

Let's understand the real impact through some of the incidents that changed people's lives who were living in contentment and peace, but were uprooted by industrialization. A large portion of farmland globally is today taken by either urbanization or industrialization. Although industries have the potential to produce at a much faster pace, but the real nourishment is still being produced and provided by the farmers and that too small farmers, but still there's very less support being provided to them. If we put things into perspective through numbers, small farmers today in the modern world are responsible for producing more than 80 percent of the food in the non-industrialized countries. The impact of industrialization is huge, especially on the small tribes, farmers, colonies and small countries as well who were content with whatever they were doing to fulfil their populations. But the compulsion to walk with the global ecosystem has forced many of them to become slaves of the new systems being created through industrialization.

If we look closely, we can see with some bit of clarity that there was the need of survival first for the early humans and to maintain that survival and make things easier they lived together and supported each other, even if it was for their own selfish motive. When survival became easier and people got time to think they started thinking about security and comfort. This was the origin of desire, which further triggered the whole cycle of evolution, struggle and ongoing misery. Need for survival gave rise to the desperation of collective living, which then triggered desire for security and comfort, these desires were followed by human actions to achieve them in form of goals and the achievement of goals were the real outcomes which further were followed by more desire and the vicious cycle continues. If observed and analysed closely, it clearly reflects the tangled web of desperation, desire, misery that defines the human experience and that tells us that there's no ultimate goal which humans have been searching and pursuing for numberless years now. The real meaning and happiness lie in the journey itself, in each and every moment in which there are sorrows, happiness, challenges, struggle and collective triumph and defeat as well. By embracing all of these, humans can really experience the ultimate truth of life.

Chapter 3

THE WEB OF CHALLENGES WITH GROWTH AND EVOLUTION – "IS IT ALL WORTH IT?"

The industrial revolution was a big change for the whole humanity. The rise of new machines, factories, and the new ways of working for the people really transformed the society in many ways. People started realizing that they have entered into a new phase of evolution which was pretty different from the older times where they had to spend a lot of time putting manual labour. But it was not an easy transition, as it brought many difficulties for the people who used to work and live in a very different environment. They were free earlier with their choices of work and they tend of work for the benefit of others and themselves. When the industry's first grew, the very first change was the shift of mindset of humans. Group of people started thinking very differently as they wanted to lead and establish control. Thus, the whole concept of governance and control came into existence. Humans started naming the resources for their own selfish objectives. The resources which nature provided for the living beings were labelled with price tags and were closed in artificial boundaries that humans created. What started with the **"just need"** of survival slowly started becoming an obsession to control and capture everything that's available to exploit by the strongest. Human evolution put them on the forefront of everything with their intelligence and ability to control. **"When humans became selfish?"**, was a "never asked question". Urbanization needed more people and these were now becoming resources as everything else. People started migrating from rural territories to urban areas as the industrialization offered them the dream of better lives. An urban dream was shown to people that had made life more comfortable with easy and all-time access to basic necessities in unlimited quantity.

Industrialization started with an intention or we can say a mission to serve the humanity, but it became an endless race where people started chasing the new dreams of making their lives more comfortable. With more people chasing these dreams, cities started becoming crowded with people, as they started shifting from rural areas to cities and thus this required more industries to open-up to provide for everyone. This soon became an opportunity and obsession for select few who then started the race of capitalism, where productivity and growth became the key vehicles of moving forward and there was no looking back. Under capitalism, cities grew further and it started engulfing the surrounding areas as well and when all this was happening, the entire natural environment suitable for humans was getting destroyed with increasing levels of air, water and soil pollution. What started as a way to create more jobs and boost the economy turned into an endless race of making more money, that often ignored the harm to environment. If we look at our cities, we can see the air filled with smoke, rivers are polluted with industrial waste and land is getting spoilt with chemicals. The desire of more profit over everything else has led to big problems, not just for the environment but also for the people living in that environment.

The story of challenges of the pre-industrial era could be an interesting part to add as a connection here and some might argue that life was hard before industrialization as it was marked with various hardships and those hardships prompted the need for change that finally triggered the rise of industrialization. The agrarian lifestyle was more in harmony with nature, but it presented significant challenges and made life difficult for people. There was dependence on weather conditions and seasonal cycles. Conditions such as floods, pests etc. sometimes led to famine and widespread suffering, which meant constant uncertainty about the food supply, leading to malnutrition and sometimes starvation as well. As, in the pre-industrial era, the agriculture was the main source of production and survival of people, the work was pretty labour intensive. People used to work from dawn to dusk doing various tasks such as ploughing fields, planting crops, taking care of the livestock. The absence of tools and machinery always led to physical exhaustion that was a common part of life. The struggle was more taking toll on people's health and leaving very little time for leisure or any education. There was no change in the profession of people born in a family, as children had to follow the footsteps of their ancestors and continue in the same profession. When class system emerged, it kept little to no room of change of status and class, thus forcing people to get stuck with the same class and status. Few who established their positions of control as landowners were at benefit and others used to live under their control and on their mercy. Health and education were a luxury for those who were working as labourers under the landowners. With increasing spread of diseases such as smallpox, tuberculosis, and cholera and limited medical knowledge the mortality rate was pretty high among the entire population. There was lack of sanitation in densely populated areas leading to frequent outbreaks of the infectious diseases. With all these challenges and much more, industrialization was seen as an opportunity to bring more security, safety and comfort.

The story of challenges and people struggling with all these challenges started working on bringing change and the whole human society worked together to drive this change that brought in the industrialization. Till now, some were seen as those, who were in position of power and control and some were really the followers. But if looked closely, all these were equally working towards the same goal which was decided by some and agreed and followed by the others. So, there's nothing to blame on anyone as humans as a society is the one to blame for this massive change that ultimately originated with a quest to find more happiness, comfort, security, safety and all that which was a challenge in the beginning. One the key triggers for industrialization was **the need for efficiency**. This efficiency was required everywhere to increase the overall production of goods and things that people needed. Traditional methods of creating goods were there but they were so slow that having to produce more goods would require significant effort and time. With evolution and increasing population people wanted more goods in less time that demanded efficiency in production. The industrialization enhanced the overall process of production by adding that efficiency in the manufacturing process. Also, with increasing population people needed stable incomes. As the process of manufacturing shifted to industries, the local workers moved to industries in need of work and they wanted more stable income to secure their lives. Also, urban areas promised the workers an improved lifestyle filled with comfort, security and steady income. Soon, cities became the major hubs of economic activity and cultural exchange, offering a very dynamic environment where people were offered ample opportunities of choice along with an improved lifestyle. "**Artificiality**" took over and became the key ingredient of human's life.

This entire journey of transition was not an overnight change, it was a gradual process that was driven by multiple forces including – necessity, opportunity, desires, greed etc. With new inventions and discoveries, humans put together the foundation of industrial age. There was rise of factories everywhere as they became the new centres of production, replacing the small hand-workers and small house units. The factories centralized production under one roof, where large number of workers were employed to operate huge machineries in a coordinated way. The new production model enabled economies of scale and increased the overall production thus driving the rapid growth of industries such as textile, steel, coal mining etc. The industrialization transformed the economies creating wealth and opportunities, attracting investments and fuelling further growth. There were new markets and expansion of trade in these new markets that drove the economic expansion and increased prosperity.

While industrialization brought in significant transformation and advancements in the human society, it also led to exploitation and further intensified the power struggle that was already there and reshaped the societies. When industrialization took over, everyone wanted to have the power and control with them, thus the pursuit of same caused many more factories to open and those with little wealth also started opening up smaller units and supporting the growth and productivity journey. With all this in action, the demand for cheap labour rose as smaller units needed labour that can work on lower wages which led to exploitation of humans as they were now just resources to fulfil the dreams of wealthy ones. Those with little to no wealth, i.e., those labelled as poor class were the victims of this entire new phase of human evolution. Women and children were also pulled into this and they worked long hours in harshest conditions for a minimal payout. Irrespective of the unit size, factories were often unsafe for the workers with little to no concern for worker's safety and health. The unending pursuit of profit and wealth by the factory owners meant an unending struggle for the poor masses. The child labour is the darkest aspect of industrialization, as even younger children of age 10 or less get employed in factories, mines, and mills where they are forced to work long hours and are paid very less and sometimes even unpaid as well. This whole process of pursuit of power, wealth and control led to the concentration of wealth, as the industrialization saw the emergence of a new class of wealthy people called "industrialists", who earned and collected great wealth and fortunes. This concentration of wealth caused significant economic disparity, with some elite controlling huge resources while majority of people, "the ordinary ones", lived in poverty. This gap between the rich and poor widened, causing social tensions and unrest across the history.

Then comes the real question **"while all this was happening, why there was no framework created to curb or put a check on this?"**. The simple answer to this is **"the human greed to accumulate more and keep surplus for coming generations"**. For establishing control and keeping a check on the ordinary, there's a governance structure that was put in place. This so-called governance structure was created with an intent to establish balance in the society, ensuring that people get rewarded for their efforts and contribution equally and there's no concentration of wealth anywhere in the society. With growing industrialization, governments became a key player in playing a supporting role by providing the required infrastructure, creating policies that favoured the industrial growth, and the whole governance structure became one sided neglecting the interest of workers. They built roads, supported establishing new banks and financial institutions to further support industrial expansion. This whole support helped the elite class and further contributed to the exploitation of labour and deepening class divide resulting in concentration of wealth.

The growing struggle was evident for those who were being "ordinary" and were controlled and exploited. This never changed and is still the same story with few in the position of control and rest just being ordinary and followers. There were many narratives that were created to support industrialization and much of the narrative later focused more on accumulation of wealth and comfort for select few. A journey which started with an intent to provide for everyone took a route of greed, selfish motives and evil aspirations to be in the position of power and establish more control on those who can follow without questioning. As mentioned earlier, there was class divide being created in the society and the class divide meant multiple groups which were having different lives and their roles were different in the society, some enjoyed the power along with the ones who were elite and some just watched them in desperation. The story for any common person never changed and the struggle continues till date. **Why there's so much of struggle for a common person is the main question that crops in the mind?** Let's get a little bit deeper into it.

When the first seeds of industrialization were sown, it was actually a few who came up with the idea that they can change things for good. Was it the real intention? The answer is – "May be". But the real intention was the aspiration to achieve more and be more comfortable. So, the real struggle is about making life more secure and comfortable. But since the resources were in their most raw form and to make them usable, there was need to bring others together in it, as the work was not a "one-man-show", it required physical and mental work. So, these select few created a narrative and the narrative was "growth and prosperity". It resonated well with others, as everyone was in need for a secure and comfortable life. Everyone wanted to have things in life so that they can live comfortably without getting worried about maintaining a daily struggle. But the larger mass never knew what they are getting into, as it was an endless loop which they started with the "people of plan". A loop which will continue till this planet continues to breathe. With growing industrialization, people became more comfortable and they started working towards making lives even more comfortable. The work for this comfort started and everyone became a part of it. Urbanization took place and continued to grow. The result was that, people from rural areas started moving towards the urban spaces and they also started living with those aspirations. With more people in the urban areas, the cities became cramped and thus the life started becoming more competitive for people. For survival they needed more money as the expenses in these cities were pretty high and surviving with little money became nearly impossible. This became an endless chase for the ordinary person who started on a journey to live a secure and comfortable life.

As we reflect on this entire journey of evolution, the emergence of industrialization and the ongoing growth in it, one thing is evident that it all started to cater some need and the intentions were somewhat good to set out on this journey. The factories, machines, automation of tasks made life easier by saving us from challenges and struggles of manual labour. The real hope however was that the technology would lead to a very different and new era for humanity where human potential would flourish, and everyone would be a beneficiary from all these evolutionary changes and advancements. The initial years of struggle and change sowed a seed, a dream that appeared quite within reach and there was great optimism towards the future. But, as the industrialization progressed, the reality that emerged was pretty different. The focus shifted towards **"efficiency and profit"** and this drive for **"efficiency and profit"** started overshadowing the initial promise of making human life better.

Human greed became the root of everything that followed this progression and evolution towards **artificialism**. The few in the position of power and control who owned the factories and the wealth started prioritizing their own profit and gains over the well-being of masses. The powerful industrialists earned vast fortunes, while the workers, labourers and the ordinary men and women who worked and toiled in the factories, witnessed just little improvement in their lives. The journey of freedom became an endless cycle of hard work and very small payouts. The journey started with a promise of experiencing freedom and prosperity, but the ordinary found themselves caught up in a material cage of desires with all the wealth owned by a select few. The dreams of a better, secure and comfortable life were shattered and the ordinary humans became witness to the harsh reality where exploitation and suppression became the new normal. This normal was filled with long hours of work for the workers in very dangerous conditions, with little wages that were barely enough to survive.

There was an inherent belief that this whole transformation with technology would be serving the humanity. But the whole thing twisted on its own and now the story is that humanity is serving the demands of technology and a few wealthy who are at the forefront of taking this whole endless race forward for their own selfish objectives and benefits. There was great potential in this industrial age to liberate people and make their time free for other creative works, but it created a system full of loopholes and corruption controlled by a handful. These handful started controlling the masses, making them trapped in relentless pursuit of profit, power, growth, efficiency and much more.

"Who is the victim of all this change and evolution?" If we ask this question to ourself – we will hesitate to accept that we supported all this change which didn't at all go in the direction it was intended for. The ordinary man like you and me are the real victims who are far from being freed by the industrial progress. People made fortunes and became wealthy, but they always feared the masses which supported them to build these fortunes and they amassed these fortunes for their own selfish benefits and the benefits of their future generations. The benefits were never shared which ideally should have been in form of equity in all those ventures which they created using others. That's the reason of the class divide and the emergence of rich and poor and the whole differentiation. The gap between the two widened with this growth and evolution journey, this resulted is creating unrest and resistance between people across the history and will continue till the time there's an equity for everyone in this growth and prosperity. The ordinary humans often wonder that whether industrial revolution was a step forward or a step back in the quest for a society whose foundation is based on equity.

There's a need to understand and clear the basics first. Machines were introduced to control and bring down the load of workers, increase the productivity, cater to the growing demand to serve the society better and provide more comfort that was unimaginable before. The dream was to create a world where people enjoy the fruits of technology and live a life of balance and harmony. But in this new world, the endless quest for balance and contentment has become pretty evident. Those on the working side found themselves trapped in a system that demanded more in return for very little. The dream of a better life was soon faced with the harsh reality of pursuit of material wealth that overshadowed even the basic well-being of humans. People are now left with little to no time to even enjoy the simple pleasures of life, as they are overworked all the time. This industrial era moved the whole human race on a path where the goals of success, happiness and satisfaction kept moving constantly. With every achievement, growth and expansion, the demands grew and there's a continuous need for more efficiency, more production, more profit and much more, which ultimately resulted in a cycle where finding balance was not only hard, but it was impossible.

The ordinary mass was trapped in an endless race with no finish line. The race is ongoing and people are continuously running in hope for that "one day", when they will be closer to achieving what they set themselves up for. But sadly, that one day is never going to come and the dream of satisfaction, happiness and contentment would remain a dream forever. Humans are in process of constant movement, but reaching nowhere. The more we run, the farther from goal we find ourselves. The end-result is just more stress, discontentment, disconnection and frustration. This whole dream of automation, comfort and pursuit of happiness and contentment has become a mirage, where there's just the illusion of a better future which would always remain a distant dream for everyone becoming part of this race.

There's a very important learning which needs to be taken away from this whole journey covered so far and still continuing. The learning is – **"When the progress, evolution, growth is driven by greed and the pursuit of more, then it can never lead to happiness and fulfilment."** This will only lead to a world where balance can't be attained and people keep on chasing something they can never really achieve. The biggest challenge for the human race now is to find an exit from this endless cycle of pursuit, to create a society which was the real dream when everything started. The society where growth and progress are not measured through accumulation of wealth, but by the well-being, happiness and satisfaction of each and every member of society.

Chapter 4

THE CHASE CONTINUES IN DIFFERENT FORM – "ARE WE STUCK WITH ILLUSION?"

Similar to the two sides of a coin, humans had different perspectives during various stages of evolution. Some converted their observation and intelligence into execution of key projects which they thought would be relevant to gain control and power on this planet. They put their heart and soul into these projects and created avenues of growth and prosperity. Then there were others who remain ignorant, always worried about **"just the day"** of survival. They followed those few who executed and led the whole transformation. **Why such differentiation between similar beings of same race?** The reason is **"motivation"**. The group who used their intelligence was motivated towards security, creation, growth, prosperity and much more. There was a continuous motivation to work towards creation of new things that could be helpful in making life more comfortable, secure and worth living. Now the question comes – what about the others, who were not pursuing this growth path. Either they were not motivated or they were too busy in ensuring their survival that their whole time and energy went there. Some might argue that it was completely based on intelligence, but the real underlying phenomenon was only **"continuous growing motivation"** to ensure the survival and make life more secure.

During the process of evolution, the whole journey of transformation was not easy. It was filled with challenges. During this process, humans unintentionally started destroying their own natural habitat. The industrialization era brought in challenges such as increasing pollutants in air and water that ultimately impacted the nature. Initially, it wasn't a concern as the amount and intensity of pollution was not huge. But with increasing number of factories to cater to the growing demands of population, the impact of pollution started growing. Today when we look around, we see many countries struggling with this menace of air and water pollution. Growth is followed by and filled with challenges, thus every step towards the growth was ultimately a new step towards the new challenges. The whole industrial evolution also set the stage for **"the digital revolution"**, the very next wave of technological advancement.

Before we move further, let's have a brief look at the series of events in this entire journey of evolution, transformation and growth. The first industrialization started somewhere between the late 18th and early 19th centuries, and this marked the historical shift from the agrarian economies to industrial powerhouses, originating in Great Britain. This new era had some groundbreaking innovations, especially in the textile industry with key inventions like the spinning jenny by James Hargreaves in 1764 and water frame by Richard Arkwright in 1769. These new machines set the stage for the factory system by boosting production. The steam engine by James Watt, further revolutionized the manufacturing and transportation, that enabled faster and efficient movement of goods and people across places. The groundwork for modern infrastructure was laid down through advancements in iron production, pioneered by Abraham Darby, that lowered the costs and improved quality. This whole revolution brought in significant growth for economies, led to accelerated urbanization with people moving to cities for new opportunities created through the industrialization. This altered the whole societal structures, creating a new working class and further reshaping the labour dynamics.

The industrialization phase was followed by the phase of expansion. Human's idea of inventing the whole industrialization concept and turning it into a reality was the first step, which was then followed by the multiple phases of growth bringing in other aspects that can further accelerate the whole process. The late 19th and 20th centuries were the witness to the second phase of industrial revolution, where the work further progressed into the direction of more advancements and expansion. This second phase allowed the spread of this whole concept of industrialization beyond the Britain to other parts of Europe and North America, with these regions witnessing the widespread adoption of electricity, transforming the production processes and the normal daily life of humans. Various industries flourished such as steel, chemicals, fertilizers that had significant impact on agriculture and manufacturing. Internal combustion engines brought in another wave of transformation leading to the birth of automobile industry, that significantly revolutionized the transportation. Communications industry contributed in connecting the world thus making it possible that people can communicate with each other across locations and geographies. The whole world shrank in terms of connectivity with the advent of communications industry. This whole revolution started with one idea that gave birth to the few industries in the beginning, and this was followed by the origin of multiple other industries across regions and geographies, that ultimately reshaped the economies and societies across the world.

When we look into history and start exploring the origin of various key industries that originated and revolutionized the whole human evolution, we become witness of various facts such as – different industries originated across different regions, the industrial revolution spread across the world from one location to another, people started working and acquiring new skills so that they can benefit from the whole process of industrialization. Let's understand the key reasons that why different regions contributed towards the emergence and growth of varied industries. There were multiple reasons for this such as natural resources availability, geographical advantage, existing skills and other socio-economic conditions. Since different countries has access to different natural resources and this abundance of resources played a key role in determining the type of industry that can be developed. As an example, the abundance of coal and iron ore in Britain supported the growth of textile, iron and steam engine industries; Germany became a leader in chemical and pharmaceutical industries due to abundance of minerals and chemicals; industries like steel, oil, agriculture flourished in the United States due to vast natural resources including coal, oil and fertile land. Similarly, the existing skills and knowledge available in the region was also a big determining factor that supported the rise and growth of industries. As an example, traditional wool and textile production laid the foundation for industrialization of textile industry in Britain; craftsmanship and academic research in chemistry and engineering enabled Germany to support the rise and growth of chemical and heavy machinery industries; innovation and entrepreneurship allowed advancements in mass production techniques in select key industries such as automotive and electrical industries in the United States.

The above discussed factors were not the only ones that supported the emergence and growth of different industries across different regions. There were other factors on the demand side of the equation as well that spurred growth, as specific products had more demand in one region than the other that led to the growth of that specific industry in that region. As an example, rapid urbanization in the Britain created a demand for affordable, mass-produced goods, driving the development of textile industry; rapid population growth created a demand for transportation, leading to the growth of railroad and automobile industries in the United States. There was support from the government with policies and economic strategies that further influenced the industrial development across different regions as per the local demand, skillset, culture etc. If we look closely, we can see that the whole industrialization was a complex process emerging from the interplay of human emotions and aspirations for economic growth. The whole process started at its core with a desire for security, stability, growth, progress, prosperity and relentless pursuit of more – **"the web of surplus"**. Humans started this process with the convergence of exploitation of natural resources, emergence of technological innovation, desire for economic growth and entrepreneurship, and this whole process laid down the foundation of this industrial age.

The origin of industrialization started with a need to serve the demand of growing population. As the needs of people were growing and there were not sufficient skilled hands to produce enough for all, this gave rise to the era of industrialization. There were other underlying intentions as well such as freeing-up people from their physical labour, machines taking over the work and thus creating better environment for the humans so that they can enjoy their leisure time with their families in the nature. The whole story of industrialization was created around this narrative. But soon after industrialization, the darker side of human ambition was unveiled. As the industries grew, the human desire for accumulation and need for surplus grew even more. The desire for control led to the exploitation of not only resources, but also the human beings as well. The continuous pursuit of profit overshadowed any other purpose that was there when it all started. All the noble intentions, ethical considerations took a back seat and the growth and expansion of industrialization took over, where it was all about more and more profit. Those with money and power started controlling and exploiting others who were in need of that power and control. This whole progress and process highlighted the dual nature of human emotion, where on one hand there was drive for innovation and improvement, while on the other side, there was greed, selfishness and evil intentions to accumulate and take it all together to establish more control. This whole progress also harmed the ecological balance as well. In need for more, humans started exploiting the natural resources and creating more artificial things that they started accumulating. So, ultimately the journey which was started to provide harmony, balance and equality turned into an endless chase for power, control and "need for more. This resulted in imbalance in the society and the environment as well. The natural habitat ultimately turned into an artificially created hostile ecosystem.

A little introspection tells us that the whole foundation of this journey was "**greed**". The greed that was sparked when humans started creating artificial goods to serve their needs. The greed for making and accumulating more converted into an endless chase that's continuing and will continue till this greed turns into a disaster for the whole humanity. Human emotions are very strong and humans have the ability to work according to their emotions. Initially when the journey to fulfil the needs started, there was great excitement and optimism. But soon when the new era took over the negative impact of industrialization became evident giving rise to disillusionment. With greed, other emotions such as comparison, jealousy, differentiation and the quest for dominance and more material wealth added fuel to fire. The technological advancements continued to grow across nations with a continuous discontent and competition. This whole journey also revealed a very complex relationship between the human emotions, aspirations and actions that turn those aspirations into reality.

As we became witnesses of human greed in the above paragraphs. Let's talk a little more about the human emotions. Industrialization was initially started as a path of progress and prosperity, but soon it revealed the darker side where exploitation, comparison, greed, differentiation and much more became common. The continuous drive to overperform the competition and build greater fortunes eventually led to the unnecessary proliferation of many industries, fulfilling the ever-growing demands and desires rather than the basic essential needs. **"Why this expansion happened and what supported this expansion?"** This was supported by the human emotions of greed, comparison and need for surplus. There were not any unmet basic needs that supported this expansion, but there were desires that took over, there was competition to dominate others that supported this expansion. The result of all this is visible today where there's no real value being delivered in meeting the basic needs. Whereas there's more focus on creating products to serve the superficial needs or desires that were created with an intent to compete and win over the competition. This has become an endless race for wealth and power.

Some might argue that with increasing population, these additional industries created more jobs and generated more employment that ultimately did a lot good for people who are engaged in these industries earning wealth for them and their families. But, let's go back to our basic question of needs and the narration to serve those needs, the real objective of industrialization. If we put all this together, we can easily conclude that humans started with an intent to serve the basics, but they somehow got confused and entangled in the web of desires that stemmed from the roots of basic needs. But these desires were not required to be served with same level of urgency and criticality. Those who wanted to establish control got the opportunity to create more jobs so that they can fulfil their desire for control and satisfaction, which was not genuinely necessary for others. Industrialists and corporate leaders got an opportunity to expand their influence and improve their status by creating crucial roles that gave a false sense of creation of employment opportunities, but hardly added any value and contribution to the societal growth and progress. This created a workforce that was engaged in activities that gave a sense of power to those on the top, but didn't add to any meaningful economic or social development.

When we look at the corporate organizations, industries that have flourished over many decades now, we can clearly see that there are lot of industries that are there with specific purpose. As an example, the financial sector especially in the areas of investment banking, has created many roles that help and support in the concentration of wealth and power without adding any tangible value to the society. Not only just industry sectors, but the problem is evident within the established organizations as well. The middle management roles within large corporations have very similar issue. It offers a sense of hierarchy and control over the junior layers and roles, rather than adding any meaningful contribution to the real productivity or innovation. Such roles and designations are created just to satisfy the egos of those up in the hierarchy and in position of power and control. There's no real or genuine economic or social need or purpose which is filled through these roles, instead such roles serve the desires of the management controlling the organization.

Industrialization evolved, corporates expanded, they wanted people to keep on consuming more so that consumerism could be sustained. In this pursuit, anything and everything which was meaningful for society took a back-seat and whatever helped boosting the consumption became the top priority for the management of large corporates. As what mattered to them was the profit and growth year over year, so that they can keep growing, creating more employment, more false narratives and roles to keep people busy. There's an old saying – **"look busy do nothing"**. These roles and organizations are a good example of this where people are hired to do something which hardly make any sense but they are doing it to earn their living. Corporates get a sense of control and establishment and people who get employed get jobs. So, with more such roles there's a false sense of employment being created. More money, more salaries mean more consumption. So, these people who work for these corporates earn money from them and then spend this money on the goods being created in their factories. So, ultimately, they are trapped in a cycle which gives them a false sense of pride, security and safety. But the reality is that they have become a part of this unfulfilling cycle or journey which is never-ending.

The reality is that people are hardly worried about pursuing any meaningful work, because they are trapped in this unfulfilling web of desires. They have been forced to become victims of consumerism, and desire more than they can actually consume. The basic needs are not a challenge anymore for anyone today, but the desires are unlimited and to fulfil those the money will always be less. Thus, people are trapped in the unmeaningful work that would hardly create any value for them and the society. Then there are industries that help supporting this whole narrative. As an example, the advertising industry promotes the unnecessary consumption by triggering the desires and needs through advertisements, where none of such need existed before, thus creating a culture of materialism. Materialism has become the central focus of the world around us today. Companies and corporations are worried about increasing their profits, they want people to buy more from them so that they can keep on increasing their revenue numbers, profit margins and thus alluring their investors. Almost every industry today has got the single objective and priority and that's profit over person. If we look at the pharmaceutical industry, the focus is on profit rather than getting worried about the patient's well-being. Examples such as opioid crisis driven by companies like Purdue Pharma, clearly reflects the intentions and the shift from the societal value to profits. All this points towards a landscape that's become more hostile and profit-driven, where initial objective of improving human lives and societal progress is overshadowed by the endless pursuit of wealth, power and control.

Industrialization had significantly impacted the environment and the overall consequences have been disastrous. The endless chase for growth and profits have resulted into widespread pollution, depletion of natural resources, and an overall large damage to the environment. Industrial activities and resultant residuals as part of these activities have polluted the air, water and soil, causing severe health risks and damage to the biodiversity. Depletion of natural resources such as oil and minerals have not only exhausted the key essential reserves but has caused the environmental destruction including deforestation and loss of habitat.

Humans fear isolation and they don't want to be alone. They always want company of others, if not humans then things, but they want the company. Human want to run away from the internal loneliness. The story of evolution highlights the initial struggle that humans faced and they started living and working together for survival in the most dangerous ecosystems where predators were always in search of human flesh. Once the humans learnt the art of being together, they started forming tribes, colonies, societies, cities, countries and the journey goes on. In this entire journey of evolution, the change and transformation from one stage to another gave rise to a number of new ideas that led to the creation of the whole artificially managed ecosystem that humans created to establish their control on this planet. Industrialization is a part of this change and transformation, that allowed humans to work towards the creation of things that they can use to establish control not only on the ecosystem but also on each other as well. Humans like company, but they also like differentiation and being in the position of authority. This same feeling led the various changes that industrialization brought. People went on to establish positions of authority, establish control over others so that they can utilize their energy, time and effort for their own benefit.

It was not an easy journey to cover and reach whatsoever far, humans have reached. But the whole journey is filled with struggles for some and luxuries, comfort for others; miseries for some and happiness and freedom for others; exploitation for some and being in the position of control for others. If we look around at the society today, there is so much we have achieved through the industrialization and further advent of internet, digital transformation and much more. But the real question is still the same – **"Are humans really free as a society and have they achieved the state of evolution for which the whole journey was started?"** When humans look around today, what they see is an artificial cage filled with all luxuries and comforts. There is a struggle every single day, the only difference is that the state of struggle is a bit different and to some extent the struggle has increased, as the world is grappling with multiple challenges due to the selfishness of humans. What's achieved is significant, but what was intended to be achieved is entirely different? A common man today wakes up to this hostile world filled with luxuries, struggle, miseries, comfort, security and much more. They need to think through with clarity that what's their real need and the real need was and still is just covering the basics which includes – food for everyone, a place to live to protect everyone from the hostilities of natural ecosystem, security and safety for everyone and a harmony among the entire race. The illusion of growth has taken control of human mind and the definition of growth is flawed. The real growth is established through self-control, establishing harmony among the population and with nature and getting back to the basics from where it all started. The state of achievement is good and great, but is this achievement worth celebrating is the real question to ask.

Materialism is the root of this entire growth phenomenon, as growth was never possible without – first controlling the natural resources and put them to exploitation for creation of things, second establishing an ecosystem where every single being is just a resource to fulfil the greed of others. **"Do humans need to forgo materialism?"** The answer is absolutely not, but there's a dire need to balance the emotions, needs and desires. There's need to build an understanding around the absolute necessity and desires. Humans can continue on the path of materialism and keep living the illusion of growth, but this journey will not lead to freedom, happiness and fulfilment that's much needed by them at any given time. So, there's a need to reprioritize the plans and actions and initiate work that's needed to bring in balance, harmony, and peace across the planet.

Chapter 5

Flawed Definitions of Key Emotions – Time to Redefine and Move Beyond the Façade

Emotions are the foundation of human existence that affect and influence human thoughts, actions and interactions at all levels. The journey of evolution provides significant evidence around this influence that really supported in shaping the overall structure of social existence. The sense of security was followed by pursuit of comfort and happiness that further gave rise to search for contentment and fulfilment. The initial emotion of security was based on the survival instinct of humans. Once the survival was ensured there followed another emotion which was happiness. Happiness has varied definitions based on the context in which it's defined. For someone who's survival and security are ensured, search for happiness is in accumulating wealth so that they can establish control and be differentiated and recognized in the society. For someone who's is just ensuring survival finds happiness in even smaller things such as ensuring basic needs are met with some room for surplus that provides a sense of extra security and brings in some happiness as well. In the world around us, when we look around, we see people are happy for multiple reasons and every reason is related to something they always either wanted or created a desire by looking at others who already have achieved those things, position, wealth and so on.

Emotions are multifaceted physiological states influenced or triggered through varied experiences including – physiological needs and the ability and way to serve them, the way humans express their behaviour in different situations, experiences gained through the conscious experiences. Emotions are internal triggers or signals that help humans by providing guidance and support in better decision making, provides ability to shape the complex human relationships, and help with the route map that can support with navigation in this vast world of existence. They are the gifts that can help enhance the overall life and existence. Emotions such as fear, love, anger, happiness and sadness are the basic emotions being gifted by nature as they are predominant emotions that humans don't even need any specialized learning to attain or trigger. Then there are enhancements that have resulted through the changes and transformation throughout the journey of evolution. Emotions are deeply personal and mostly shaped through personal experiences and the surrounding societal structure and ecosystem.

Emotions are like instincts for ensuring our basic survival and they often go beyond the basic needs of humans. There's a greater significance in understanding the human emotions, as there's quite a good chance that they are misunderstood and misinterpreted in different situations. If we reflect and look back at the history, there's evidence highlighting that various cultures focused on understanding the human emotions and to serve the needs better they developed different frameworks to first understand the emotions and human abilities to express them fairly and openly. In some societies, human emotions were very closely knitted with the foundational values of existence of these societies. They were attached to the communal values and spiritual beliefs that focused on bringing in harmony, equality, balance in closely connected communities. In a general sense, emotions can be viewed as being related to maintaining the basic harmony along with personal well-being of individuals as well.

During the course of evolutionary journey, humans have been the integral witness and part of many philosophies and religious frameworks such as Hinduism, Buddhism, Jainism, Islam. Out of these different religions and philosophies, the religions mostly focused on the development of the belief systems that served as a common thread for communities, societies and even countries. Religion is based on some key pillars including fear, love, service, faith, rituals and practices. When we look at some old traditional tales, we see people often connecting themselves with natural entities, things or beliefs.

Let's understand this with a small example – there's a small village that's located very close to a large mountain that's considered as sacred and none in the village or around has ever been able to climb it to the top. The villagers started developing a belief that the mountain is sacred and is a symbol of their fear and they started worshiping it as something that's greater and mightier *(difficult to climb)*. Soon, the belief turned into a deep emotion of connectedness, fear and love. Connectedness among the people with a belief that they need to serve each other's need and the mountain will provide them with its blessings, fear as the mountain was almost impossible to climb and thus considered sacred and mightier, and love as they started getting their wishes fulfilled and their village started living in harmony and people love and serve each other. Every morning when the sun rises, villagers come together to offer prayers to the mountain. Soon a temple was built in the village for people who were away from the mountain so that they can start offering their prayers in the temple and seek the blessings. Their days were filled with engagement in service of each other, helping each other with simple and complex tasks that they used to do on a daily basis, showing empathy and kindness towards each other and ensuring that no one is left behind or feeling left-out from the society. In the times of struggle and challenges, they strongly held these emotions and they realized that their belief system was really helpful in serving their needs better, making them stronger to face any challenges and hardships. Their lives started getting enriched with many different rituals, practices and events such as festivals, communal prayers, and many other traditions that can help in increasing their bonding with each other and thrive as a society that's working for the betterment of each other.

As we can clearly see and understand from the above example story that belief systems were really the foundation when it comes to religion and the key pillars of love, fear, service, rituals and faith helped societies work, live and progress together towards the common goal of harmony, happiness and overall well-being. So, when we understand these emotions being knit together into a common framework that provided pathway towards a life that humans always wanted where they want to live in harmony, work together as a group for personal and other's well-being and enrich their lives with happiness and peace, then we realize that they are so deeply connected. But somewhere in the modern world, the definitions of these emotions have changed and diluted in a sense that they often are disconnected from the foundational principles.

Religions started losing charm and slowly the influence also started getting lost over time, that led to a gap in the principles and guidance that once taught people the art of life. While religions were losing their charm and influence, the gap created was clearly seen by some and they started adding philosophies to influence people and the whole trend of spiritual leaders started to emerge. They offered new promises to people stating that they would guide and help in getting back to the foundational definitions of morality, fulfilment, purpose and much more. As an example, Sidhartha Gautama introduced Buddhism and the philosophy focused on four key pillars called as four noble truths and eightfold path. The whole philosophy encourages detachment from the material desires and focus on moving towards internal peace and contentment. The story of Sidhartha narrates the sea-change that happened suddenly in his life while he was in his adulthood. His father had a lot of aspirations and dreams for him, but one incident changed the whole path of his life. When he came to know about the miseries of life, despite being kept in an environment which was full of happiness, material pleasures and luxuries of life, he immediately understood that he needs to act and do something about it and then the whole story is about the struggles he had to face to finally achieve the spiritual enlightenment which led him to spread the same to others so that they can also learn and lead a life which is away from the miseries of life and away from the material illusions of the world. The philosophy introduced by Gautam Buddha focused on highlighting that suffering is caused by the desires and attachment. So, the elimination of desires and attachment is the path of attaining a state of Nirvana, which is the state of ultimate peace and liberation from the cycle of material traps *(the philosophy mentions this as liberation from rebirth).*

Other spiritual leaders such as Swami Vivekananda also advocated the path of simple living, spiritual growth with an emphasis on the true happiness that can't be achieved through the material pleasures and fulfilment of these material desires. True happiness is achieved through simplicity and that comes from within through peace and contentment with self. Teachings of Vivekananda were derived from the Hindu mythological texts and guidance of guru, Sri Ramakrishna Paramhansa. The teachings emphasized the importance of self-realization and unity with the existence. He also advocated the similar philosophy of attaining happiness through inner peace and contentment, as material desires and attachment traps the individual into an endless pursuit of material pleasures that ultimately lead to frustration and discontentment. The teachings also focused on making people aware that they should rise above their selfish desires and act for the greater good of humanity.

Ancient Hindu mythology also highlight the significance of contentment over the material desires and pleasures. Hindu mythology text "Bhagwat Gita" elaborates on it further through the philosophy of "Nishkama Karma", that means working without having desire for outcome or result. So, there's no attachment to results, but still the individual is focused on acting as needed to fulfil his or her duties. There's a story in Hindu mythology about a great king called King Janka. The story of King Janaka highlights that despite having immense riches, the king was not having any attachment to the material wealth and he was very focused on fulfilling his spiritual duties. This illustrates that true contentment is not in material wealth, but attaining peace with self and working selflessly throughout the life. A similar other story of "Sudama", a poor Brahmin who was living in extreme poverty once visited his friend "Krishna" who was wealthy and was capable of helping anyone. But Sudama didn't ask anything from Krishna, he just met Krishna and came back without showing any desire or request. But when he returned back to his house, he realized that Krishna has provided him with riches without even being requested to do so. This highlights that Sudama's humility and self-contentment led Krishna to reward him with wealth.

But all these philosophies which emerged over time and gained prominence, started conflicting with the traditional doctrines and they also were not in agreement with new emerging perspectives. This conflict between the philosophies and religious beliefs led to another level of emotional complexity where people were really confused and started questioning the ideologies. There arose another desire for more clarity and getting away from this confusion and this further led to emotional chaos causing erosion of societal pillars that these philosophies were meant to strengthen. As an example, the conflict between the traditional Hindu caste system and principles of Buddhism led to significant societal disturbance in ancient India. Similarly, the popularity and spread of other spiritual principles such as Sufism in Islam, that laid emphasis on personal connection with the divine over adhering to the doctrine, raised conflicts but at the same time also further enriched the spiritual foundational pillars.

When humans were living as wanderers in the predatory ecosystem, they were worried about their food and safety. Securing food for themselves was the prime objective and once they achieve it, they would be content, this contentment can be related to happiness as well. So, that means humans become happy when they were able to secure food for their physical strength and survival. Over time, it became easier to survive and get food. Soon, they started to accumulate food as well so that they don't have to hunt or go in search of food every time. Let's understand the underlying emotions and thought process behind all this. Prime need was food and that was getting fulfilled. As and when they got hungry, they got in search of food and get it with significant effort. The sense of getting and securing meal to serve their hunger gave them a sense of happiness and contentment. So, the happiness was related to just getting food for survival. Soon, they realized that the process was pretty taxing and they started gathering food for storage so that they can go on it easy for some days and then some months and so on. This desire to accumulate became the next prime objective for them now. The sense of achievement and happiness was not in securing food anymore as getting food was becoming easier and the focus was on accumulating surplus for coming times. So, the happiness and contentment now shifted to this accumulation. The more they got, happier they felt. Soon, this process became easier and humans learnt to cover up the basic need of food and storage. Once this became easier, they were ready for the next challenge and the journey continues till today. Today people are not finding happiness in covering up the basics such as food, shelter and clothes. For some it's true today as well because we have made the world a place where classification, division and class system has really taken over the well-being and harmony in the overall society.

If we understand this closely, we can clearly see that there's a desire first which triggered human action to search for food. Once the desire got fulfilled, there's a sense of fulfilment and then happiness. But as the process became easier, another thought invaded the human mind and that thought created another desire and the happiness and contentment was now shifted to the new desire. Eventually, what's happened is humans started becoming slaves to their own desires, and these desires were being controlled by thoughts which came through observation of the needs and search for more happiness and get rid of any mundane activity in life. Today, humans have really become the victim of their own desires and the cloud of desires has become so dense that there's no clarity anymore on what should be done to get rid of this cycle of unfulfillment, dissatisfaction, discontentment and frustration. The world has become a place where there are people who are struggling with their basic needs and then there are people who have surplus and still unfulfilled as they are searching for some meaning and purpose in life. This is a result of this continuous evolution that people are stuck with the **"next big thing desire"** internally.

Materialism is an illusion which is being created to be chased by the human beings. **"Who created it? Is it us or is it our desires or our thoughts that triggered these desires?"** The answer is not that plain and simple. It needs a very close observation and understanding of the human behaviour. Humans are intelligent beings and that's what separated and distinguished them from other beings in nature. They always knew what's required for survival and they tried everything possible to attain that. So, the survival instinct was the inherent attribute that pushed them to do whatever possible. Once survival was ensured, the quest for other things began and then others and so on. We can clearly understand this with an example of today's modern world. When a person achieves the basic, he moves on to pursue other luxuries of the world as he can't stop at basics. The biggest reason is the emptiness which is inside the humans. Everyone is trying to fill that emptiness thus we see people hardly have any patience today. The more we achieve, the hungrier we become.

So, can we say that we have got it all wrong and the quest for fulfilment was not a chase for materialism which world is celebrating today. We have everything available at our fingertips today with technology making it all more convenient for us with every passing decade. The more we have achieved, the more disturbance we have created in the whole living ecosystem. The hunger has grown so much that world is grappling with challenges of basics again, countries are trying to establish control over each other, everyone wants to become superior to others and all this pursuit is becoming endless now. In this quest, humans have destroyed the natural ecosystem and are continuously destroying it. Once who used to live at the mercy of predators in the natural environment has changed role today and has become the predator for nature. Where it all points to? - is a cycle of existence which is continuously moving and with-it roles are changing, and with changing roles the sense of achievement is shifting away forcing to think that what ultimately is being chased and where all of this is going to lead the whole humanity and existence towards.

So, we see the emotions are directly linked to desires and the desires are the result of our thoughts. When thoughts trigger some desire about something we want or need, the desire then further activates the emotional responses such as happiness, sadness, excitement, fear and so on depending on the result of our actions which we take in the direction of that desire. As an example, the thought of achieving something which is part of our long-term goal will trigger the desire for success and this desire would further lead to emotions of motivation, anticipation etc. Contrary to it, if we fear losing anything which appears very important to us this would result in creation of a desire to prevent the loss, which is turn would lead to anxiety or fear.

The cycle of desires tells us that something is not right and the way we define these emotions today is not exactly the right way of looking at them. In an ideal scenario, there needs to be a balance between the desires and the actions in response to these desires. Because the endless cycle of desires is really a trap for humans which in the end leads to illusion of happiness which is always like a dream which vanishes as it gets closer to reality. So, in essence the way we are defining these emotions today is not right and the definitions are getting flawed. This is resulting in constant pursuit of more material possession for happiness and fulfilment which have become a distant dream. There's continuous chase happening making people believe that more they will pursue material possessions, the happier they would become. But all this is not bringing in lasting happiness and thus after sometime they start feeling empty and frustrated again. These flawed definitions of emotions are not helping in any sense, instead they are creating more misery for people and the whole living ecosystem is paying the price for it.

Everyone is after something and that something is never achieved in their lifetime. The chase continues till they reach their deathbed and the late realization hits in spreading salt on the unhealed wounds of endless pursuit and chase that has made them tired and helpless. The continuous chase for material happiness is like an aimless chase where nothing is going to be achieved at the end, but still the chase continues with all the participants looking at each other for acknowledgement that what they have achieved is really worth celebrating. The ultimate goal of achieving harmony is left far behind in this endless pursuit because our understanding of true happiness has distorted.

Let's understand what we discussed above through some interesting stories. As an example, there was a King from Green mythology, King Midas. He was granted a wish that anything and everything he touches would turn into gold. Initially, he was pretty excited with the wish, but soon he hit the realization that this wish was no less than a curse, as he wasn't able to eat, drink and even touch his loved ones or else they would turn into gold. His desire for unlimited wealth and luxuries of life led to this misery and curse. This story clearly demonstrates that if your desires are left unchecked, it can lead to emotional disaster. In the modern world, people are running behind material desires and they are losing on many valuable moments of life which they can utilize otherwise to attain peace, contentment and happiness. Consumerism has trapped many, who keep on buying stuff, gadgets, items etc. with a hope that all these things will provide them happiness. However, the satisfaction which they get is momentary and fades away quickly, leading to an endless cycle of desires, temporary pleasures and ultimate misery.

Another interesting story is about a monk and a fisherman. The monk once met the fisherman who was complaining about the struggles and hardships in life. The monk suggested him that he should sell his boat and fishing net and buy a small piece of land for farming. He acted on the advice and bought a small piece of land. Soon, he became a successful farmer and his material desires started rising. Now he wanted bigger farm, bigger house, more men working for him and more material wealth and all the luxuries of life. These desires made him stressful and discontent with life again. The initial advice from monk was focused on having a simple life and attain simplicity and inner peace. But he instead focused on attaining material wealth and possessions causing unhappiness and discontentment. This story pretty much reflects what's happening in the modern society as well, where a small initial success lead people to chase more material wealth, pleasure and large ambitions that results in more stress, anxiety and discontentment moving people away from the true happiness and fulfilment.

For those who find struggle and hurdles of life as curse, they need to rethink and introspect a little bit that what they have is more than enough. There's a story about a person who was unhappy with his life's struggle and was attempting suicide. While he was standing on the edge of a mountain, a saint was passing nearby. The saint saw him and went to him asking why he is trying to kill himself. To this he replied that his life is a complete waste and there's nothing left to live for and thus he is ending his life. The saint requested him that he should rethink his decision and come with him to a place where he will get to know his real worth. He agreed after some convincing and went ahead with the saint. Saint took him to a nearby king's court and told the king the whole story. Then he said that since the king need the body parts of a healthy individual, this young individual should be a perfect fit for it. While all this was happening, the person stood there confused. The king looked towards the person and said that if you can donate your eyes, hands and other parts, you can get money for each and every part you donate. Listening to this, he cried that what kind of court is this who is demanding organs of a living person. The saint interrupted and said that you were about to die as you didn't see meaning in living and you have lost everything, then why are you worried now. You will die by doing a noble deed of donating your body parts and your family will get some benefit of your death as well. The person soon realized that the real wealth is his body through which his existence is possible on this earth, rest all is just material illusion and endless chase of materialism. This story reflects the fact that we often ignore the true wealth gifted to us and endlessly aim of things that are hardly of any value. The ultimate contentment can be attained through self-realization and self-introspection.

Chapter 6

THE ENDLESS DILEMMA – IS THE PURSUIT OF MATERIAL HAPPINESS WORTH THE TIME AND EFFORT?

The modern world is a perfect example of material pursuits which has taken priority in the minds of people. If we go back and look into ancient times, this phenomenon has been the key driver in the human life. So, it's not just now that the people are chasing material happiness, the chase began way back in the history of mankind when humans were able to fulfil the basic needs and got time to think about what next? This curiosity of what next led to the thoughts and then desires of material pursuits. Humans started exploring ways of creating things and these things in turn became their obsession and led to happiness driven by these things. The whole phenomenon evolved with the evolution of humans and today in the modern world we see this in every aspect of life. Everyone is chasing something and, in this chase, they are forgetting their freedom, peace, physical and mental wellbeing. The whole phenomenon of material pursuits has shaped civilizations and provided them with influence they wanted to create over each other. So, the emotion of control and differentiation has clouded the whole process of progression towards a better society where people can live in harmony, peace and share prosperity.

If to be put in perspective, it can be said that human existence revolves around the material happiness and that's the central theme of existence. But the agony, miseries, discontentment and frustrations brought in through this endless cycle can't be denied and ignored. An honest introspection can reveal a lot which is not right and that needs to change for the betterment of society as a whole. But, **"are humans really worried about it?"**. They are busy with this endless chase hardly finding any time to even think about their physical and mental health. Modern society has developed and provided multiple avenues of creating illusionary busyness that there's hardly anytime left to think with clarity and depth. The senses are numb, minds are clouded with illusion of artificiality and pursuit of material wealth. For those who have attained a certain level of wealth has another significant feeling or emotion and that is about the clarity and purpose in life. So, what it essentially reflects is that the point from where it all started, at the end the things roll-back to the same place, the feelings remain as they were before. The sense of emptiness, missing purpose of existence and deep agony and longing for internal satisfaction remains prominent.

The real question that stands "as-is" today is – **"Have we achieved the true freedom with all this chase thus far?"** The answer to this question is hidden inside the journey humans have covered so far. The endless pursuit of material wealth and advancements has not enabled humans to get the freedom they need the most. The freedom still remains a distant dream that everyone is longing to achieve. The desires for attaining more and gathering more possessions has led to deeper entanglements in this consumerism cycle where debt and environmental degradation have become common. Human society as a whole might have achieved technological progress and economic growth that has helped them with comfort and convenience, but on the flip side this whole progress and growth has created newer forms of dependence and inequality. So, the true freedom hasn't been achieved through this quest for material wealth and progress.

The modern world is obsessed with wealth accumulation, as humans believe that money can provide them freedom. So, the more money they earn the more freedom they will get. At the face of it, it appears true as money offers freedom from financial needs, freedom to buy and accumulate material wealth, and freedom to experience the luxuries and comfort of life. However, in reality this momentary freedom is an illusion that traps the mind with all the desires and thoughts of enjoying life. The more people earn and the more they accumulate, the more pressure they feel to maintain a certain type of life and that life comes at a cost, the cost of increasing this accumulation of wealth. With accumulated wealth comes more desires and some of the desires are triggered by the societal pressures. Let's have a look at lives of working-class people who are working tirelessly to earn and maintain a certain standard in life. They are hoping to accumulate more to attain freedom. Most successful people *(the material success)* follow the same pattern with more rigor to achieve more success in terms of accumulation of wealth and achieve a certain standard in the society. Their belief is that the more successful they become, the more freedom they would attain. But in reality, the reverse is true. As people start climbing the ladder of success, they start losing their time as most of their time and energy goes in the process of earning more. The more they acquire and accumulate, the more they desire, and this becomes an endless cycle of consumption. Modern world's reality is consumption and this consumption is not only harming people, but it's harming the nature and the whole ecosystem of existence as well. This cycle often starts with the societal pressure, the desire to differentiate from others and earn and maintain prestige. This cycle doesn't stop at just earning more, it forces people to acquire more and even those things and luxuries which are often beyond their potential earnings and wealth. This whole phenomenon triggers the cycle of endless debts which then traps people and they are bound to work tirelessly till they clear off their debts.

Modern world is a witness of stressful jobs, long working hours, ignored physical and mental health and creeping anxiety and fear of losing it all. The more people earn and acquire the more unfulfilled they feel and this unfulfillment lead to other desires and thus the cycle goes on and on. Whole human society today is caught up in an endless cycle of consumption and work. The work which in reality is not at all meaningful or of any value to the society. Humans are not only harming themselves they are harming the environment as well. The chase for wealth and so-called prosperity has taken significant toll on the environment, that in turn limits the freedom of current and future generations. The depleting natural resources, air, water and soil pollution, climate change and natural disasters are the result of overconsumption and increased industrial activity. These issues are not providing freedom instead they are limiting freedom of humans by threatening the ecosystem and resources of dependence.

As an example, increasing deforestation that's a result of increasing demand for more agriculture land and timber has impacted biodiversity and impacted many indigenous tribes and communities. The air, water and soil pollution have adverse effects on the human health and in turn it's impacting the overall wellbeing of humans and the quality of life. With increasing industrial activity and pollution, the climate across the planet is significantly impacted. As this change of climate will accelerate, natural disasters such as extreme temperature rise, rise in sea levels, melting glaciers will threaten the existence across the globe. Environmental destruction is impacting the freedom to live in a stable, healthy environment which is the basic requirement for human survival. This change is forcing the societies to allocate resources towards the correction and mitigation steps. But how proactively this change is being propagated is a critical question to answer. If these challenges continue then the planet would become unsuitable for human existence.

Environmental change is not the only challenge that exists in front of human society in the aftermath of industrial growth and progress. This pursuit for material wealth and growth has also further created social inequalities that limit and impact the freedom for many communities and individuals. The wealth is getting concentrated in the hands of a select few groups and individuals which is leading to a huge gap between people differentiating them as rich and poor. Today when we talk about progress, growth, prosperity and freedom, there are millions on this planet who don't have even enough resources to cover up their basic needs. There's a continuous struggle for people to make the ends meet and this is leading to growing frustrations, anxiety, fear and social unrest in the society which is highly polarized in wealth distribution. Let's have a look at some examples to understand this in more detail.

In the bustling large cities with good infrastructure and facilities for education, healthcare and superior resources, the lives of people are very different depending on their earnings and status. There are people who earn great fortunes and have access to almost everything including – good education, healthcare and all other luxuries of life, while there are others who belong to poor class where even the basic living conditions are not up to the mark and are below living standards. The poor class in these cities even don't have access to clean water and proper sanitization. Their children can't go to good schools and thus the level of education they get is not a par with what children of middle, upper middle and rich class get. This creates further differentiation in the opportunities they get in their lives. Poor people don't have access to good healthcare, so they are bound to go to public hospitals which are overburdened and understaffed. Whereas others belonging to the upper class have access to all the amenities including good healthcare, good infrastructure, great living conditions. People below a certain earning potential hardly even make ends meet in these cities, but they still want that they stay in these cities and work for providing good education to their children so that they can progress in their lives. There's a distant dream which everyone has, who comes to these cities.

There are enormous opportunities for the people who belong to the upper and elite class. The real question is that why such class differentiation. Some might argue that there are equal opportunities to people and some have already worked hard enough to get out of the poverty. But the question still remains unanswered that why this differentiation in the first place. Why can't there be fair distribution of facilities, opportunities, resources as that's the evolutionary dream with which humans started the journey of evolution and growth. The dream to achieve a society where everyone is equal and get equal opportunities and resources so that people can live in harmony and with freedom, appears diluted and corrupted.

With evolution and growth, the foundational frameworks set by humans started to get corrupted, as few with strength and desire to establish control amended the frameworks in their favour and the phenomenon continued and the result is the state of a modern world with everything available but people still dying of hunger, pathetic living conditions, living in poverty and misery.

Data from across the globe tells the story about the existing condition of society. In the United States, the wealth gap has been growing between the top 1% and rest of the population. Elite and wealthy enjoy special privileges and ample number of opportunities, whereas million others struggle with job security, low earnings, and limited access to healthcare and education. The situation is even worse in other developing nations across the world. The resources and wealth distribution ratio are completely skewed with few elite controlling majority wealth, while majority of population struggles to make ends meet. There's majority population that lives below poverty in many developing countries. This type of disparity in wealth and resources not only affects the people but has larger implications for the whole society. Such situations often result into social unrest, as people become frustrated with their limited opportunities and access to basic resources. The system created to bring equality, freedom and harmony remains ineffective in achieving the desired goal.

The change is very much required and it's not the responsibility of an individual or group, but it's a combined responsibility of individuals, groups, governments, corporations, institutions and all other foundational systems. A strong collective framework is required to correct the course of progress and evolution. Ethics and principles can help in bringing this change where human wellbeing is prioritized over the monetary gains. Social justice and support initiatives should aim to reduce the inequality. There are a lot of empowering stories where individuals stood for the change and brought in that change for the overall good of society and individuals.

There has been a lot of focus on girl's education and many worked for the empowerment and equal rights of the girl child.

As an example, Malala Yousafzai worked and fought for the education rights of girls in Pakistan despite being faced with significant opposition and even an assassination attempt. Her determination and firm stand turned global attention towards this issue. Her work and efforts have empowered many girls to pursue education and rise above the poverty. Her story is a great reminder of all the work which is yet required to be done in the modern world. The story also highlights the significance of prioritizing human rights and equality over economic growth and selfish gains.

Another example is of Kenya where people didn't have access to the banking to save, invest and transfer money. The M-Paisa mobile money platform revolutionized the financial transactions ecosystem, by enabling people to save, invest and transfer money to others. This innovative platform also helped many to start smaller new businesses, work on the improvement of their livelihood, and attain a sense of security and economic freedom.

There are organizations globally who are involved in building affordable houses for masses, especially those with low-incomes. E.g., Habitat for humanity in the United States works toward addressing the housing inequality through affordable houses for poor class. Such initiatives not only help people in getting a place to live but also brings in some sense of security and freedom for lower-income groups. This also highlights that real progress comes from helping and empowering others, so that they can get out of the cycle of poverty.

The chase is endless and there's an illusion at destination. This illusion sets another destination which again requires significant amount of dedication, effort and time. When someone reaches a destination, they realize that there's no fulfilment even after making it up here. Then they start looking at other ways of fulfilling their life. As an example, people moving into cities come with a dream to earn good income and utilize this income for the security and comfort of their family. Once settled in the city, they fall in the trap of material illusions like settling in that city in big houses, driving big cars, purchasing expensive gadgets, expensive holidays and vacations and so on. All this pursuit comes at the cost of their and their family's wellbeing, peace and dedicated time which they devote to earn this income which hardly serves their needs. In big cities, people buy expensive things and fall in the trap of debt and this debt trap is forever for some who never make out of it. History has taught many lessons to humans, but humans often forget these lessons and start chasing the material pursuits. In most of the mythological texts and the learnings from various guides and gurus, it has often been highlighted that the real life is worth living in the nature and spending time for something which is meaningful and beneficial for everyone around. Selfish objectives would always lead to frustration and anxiety, which in turn would lead to fear of losing security and safety. It's high time that humans bring those learnings in their life and start working towards the betterment of existence rather than chasing endless material pursuits.

While leaving this chapter and making inroads further into our journey, I would like to highlight an interesting story that teaches more about the fulfilment and peace. Once upon a time, there lived a humble fisherman named Purusha in the coastal village. His life was filled with peace and pleasure. He would wake up early in the morning and would take his boat into the blue waters of ocean. He would catch fishes as per his and his family's needs and come back to his home by mid-day. The rest of the time he would spend with his family and friends. His life was simple and filled with contentment and peace.

One fine day a businessman visited the village with family for a vacation as the nearby environment and scenic beauty was very peaceful and worth the time. While on vacation, he would often go to the sea-side and watch the fishermen go and return after catching fishes. He also watched Purusha and was intrigued with his routine. Out of curiosity, he approached Purusha and started conversing with him about the place and then about his routine. When he started enquiring into his routine, he asked that why Purusha comes back so early while others are still working to catch more fishes. He said to Purusha that if he stays longer in the sea, he can catch more fishes. To this Purusha responded that he catches fishes for meeting his family's needs so he catches enough to meet those needs. He further added that as he finishes his work earlier, he comes back and enjoy spending time with his family and friends and also gets time to relax as well.

The businessman said to Purusha, "But if you could work a little more and catch more fishes you could earn more. With that extra money, you can buy a bigger boat and also employ some fishermen for support and this will help you to create a small fishing business." He further said, "you should think about it, as the money that you can make could make your and your family's life happier, secure and peaceful". He continued, "you could get back lot of your time and you can spend quality time with your family and friends. You could retire early and enjoy all the wealth without having to put in much hard work".

Purusha was listening to the businessman carefully and after listening he said to businessman, "What do you think I am doing now?"

The businessman was surprised after hearing Purusha's reply and then he realized that Purusha already has what he is suggesting him to attain after doing all that material chase. Purusha was already leading a peaceful and fulfilled life where he was enjoying time with his family and friends. This short conversation with Purusha helped the businessman realize that despite having so much wealth, his life is filled with anxiety, stress and loads of hard work in chase of material pleasures. The businessman realized that it's important to find contentment and fulfilment in simple events and pleasures of life, focusing on relationships, and living in harmony with others on this planet.

Similar to this businessman, humans are running a race of achievement which in itself is illusion. The real achievement is not in earning more wealth and accumulating more wealth, but the real achievement is in creating healthy relationships with others, living peacefully on this planet showing gratitude for what nature has already provided.

This short story aligns with what people are busy doing in the modern world. They are trapped in the cycle of work, consumption, and desire for more. Such anecdotes challenge our thinking and force us to rethink the foundational frameworks and rethink our priorities. Material wealth is not and will never be the end-goal, instead working together for creating a better world is the journey all should aspire for taking. There's need to work towards the creation of a society where people live in harmony, work and support each other, and find life pleasures in small instances and things.

What's needed to bring harmony into the society?

Bringing harmony into the society requires fostering empathy, increase collaboration, and create a sense of community in all individuals. It also means that people should understand valuing people over possessions and keeping everyone's wellbeing on priority. Some ways to bring harmony into our lives include:

- **Practice empathy and compassion**: It's important to understand everyone's feelings and pain. When in pain, people should help each other to overcome the struggles causing this pain. Having help and support as the foundational pillars of society would help bringing empathy and compassion into practice.

- **Relationships should be the centre point of existence**: Investing time and effort in building strong relationships with not only friends and family, but also with others in the society helps in creating a strong foundation. These relationships and bonds give lasting happiness and fulfilment to all.

- **Simplification of life**: Simplifying the life with a focus on things, activities and actions that really matter for the well-being and betterment of the whole society. Leaving all the desires of accumulation and consumption would help appreciating the simple things in life.

- **Equality and fair treatment for all**: A healthy and progressive society should be inclusive enough to have equality and fair treatment for its people. Everyone should be provided with equal opportunities and should have access to the basic needs and facilities.

- **Respect nature and show gratitude**: Nature has already provided everything to all on this planet to survive with security and comfort. So, it's important to respect nature and show gratitude for what's being already provided. A healthy planet would ensure the health and well-being of its living beings.

- **Mindfulness**: It's important to learn living in the present moment and take pleasure in small joys of life. Continuously express gratitude for what's being provided around by the nature. Be aware and focused on working towards the betterment of everyone.

So, now let's get back to where we started from and try answering the question, **"Is it worth the time and effort we spend in chasing material happiness?"** What we learnt here is that it's far more important to work towards building a society which has harmony and peace among its people rather than glamorizing the pursuit of material wealth and happiness. The real happiness is in every moment, every small activity that happens in the nature, every small joy that comes our way. So, let's work towards living and promoting a life filled with gratitude, mindfulness and equality to attain real progress.

Before closing this chapter, let me tell you another interesting story of Alexander. Once Alexander went to a Sufi Saint. The saint was resting and Alexander went close and sat near him. As he sat near the saint, saint asked him a question – "Alexander! If you are alone and trapped in a desert with no idea of directions to get out and you are very thirsty. A person comes to you with a glass of water, but he would need something in return for this water. So, what would you be able to offer him in return for this glass of water."

Alexander replied that he would offer him his half kingdom. Hearing this saint said that if that person is me and I am not satisfied with your half kingdom then what would you offer. To this, Alexander replied that then I will give away my whole kingdom if I am at verge of dying with thirst. The Sufi saint smiled at Alexander and said that what's the use of tirelessly aiming for winning all the empires and killing so many people when this whole wealth of yours is not even worthy enough and it can go away for a glass of water. There are many stories like this which clearly teaches us about the experiences people had in the past and how they learnt things the hard way. We need to rethink our priorities and work towards the goals which are worth achieving and making this world a better place.

Chapter 7

THE MODERN DIGITAL TIMES – WHAT'S THERE IN STORE FOR US: HYPE OR HYPERTENSION?

Modern world is the golden avenue where there are technological advancements, sophisticated infrastructure, artificial lifestyle products and much more. The advent of digital age transformed the world significantly by bringing change in the ways of working, communicating, entertaining, shopping and overall living as well. The internet and digital age brought in the promise of making information easily accessible across the globe, making communication more efficient and making daily tasks easier and more convenient. It revolutionized the lives of people in many different ways. Today the knowledge is democratized which allows anyone and everyone to access and learn anything they want. Information is easily accessible on any topic that exists on this planet. Then there's social media that has made it easier to stay connected with friends and family. Irrespective of your location, you can connect with anyone through social media and smartphones. With accelerated online activity, many shoppers are selling online on e-commerce platforms, which in turn has made it convenient for people to do shopping and buy anything from the comfort of their homes. Applications for performing many tasks and functions have allowed people to easily accomplish their tasks e.g., entertainment, money transactions, shopping, communications and much more.

The promise with which the whole digital age started are fulfilled today. Looking around us can help us understand how technology has become an integral part of our lives. Working people use digital alarm clock to wake up at a particular time. These digital alarm clocks are synced with their calendar to ensure timely prompt. Checking emails and any social media notifications are really easier as they can be done through the smartphones. Shopping is easier that means people can order their breakfast using delivery apps on their smartphones. Talking to people in work has become easier through the collaboration applications such as Teams, Slack, What's App etc. Virtual meetings have become common to add convenience to people's lives so that they can work from anywhere. People across the globe can connect and work together though these digital advancements. Managing tasks is easier with the help of productivity apps. Finally, entertainment of choice is available on click of a button. All this highlights the conveniences of the digital era.

Technology has taken over most of the work people used to perform earlier. Today, most tasks can be accomplished through various applications on a single click. But all this has its own set of challenges and pitfalls as well. The rise of social media platforms such as Facebook, Instagram, TikTok etc., have served the need of connection among people, but on the other hand these platforms have created a culture of self-obsession. Let's understand this through a small story. There's a story from Greek mythology about a handsome youth named Narcissus. Once Narcissus went out for hunting. While hunting, he felt thirsty and he went to get some water from the river. As he bent down to get some water, he saw his own reflection and he fell in love with it. He became so obsessed with it in that very moment that he decided that the two would die as one. He stayed near the river without any sleep or food. He called to gods that why he was being denied the love that the two shared. He started to talk to his own reflection. This obsession led to his death. He eventually wasted away and died, turning into a flower that bears his name.

With the rise of increasing usage of social media, people spend most of their time online. They wake up to their smartphones and throughout the day they keep checking the social media feeds and notifications. Even while sleeping they keep checking their mobiles till, they fall asleep. Everyone has his or her own online persona. With the online presence, everyone keeps seeking validation through likes, shares, comments. There's a pursuit of good and perfect selfies, more followers, more likes and more connections. Everyone is after increasing their follower count. People are connected to so many others who they don't even know in reality. But they are busy enjoying this connectedness in their virtual world. This is similar to the obsession Narcissus had with his own reflection. The story of Narcissus serves as a caution for modern day's social media usage and the whole digital age. While there are many benefits of the social media as it serves as a medium to connect with the loved ones who live away from their homes, but on the other hand it also raises concerns of giving rise to a culture of jealousy, arrogance, and self-obsession. People are at risk of losing themselves in the pursuit of online validation. When the focus on self-image grows, it results in loss of genuine human connection, thus replacing real-life interactions with virtual ones. People who are having this self-image obsession often are in constant need to project a perfect image of themselves that sometimes can lead to anxiety, depression and loss of self-worth.

The modern world has an accelerated pace of life. People have become used to instant communication, easy and prompt access to information, and rapid delivery of goods and services. There's a growing problem of instant gratification with this rise in the pace of life. People have started losing patience and they can't wait. The wait times lead to frustration and in some situations turn them hostile. All this has led to the increased stress levels of people in the modern world. Everyday many people lose their lives due to this increased stress and anxiety, as they can't cope up with this fast-paced culture. The rise of social media and growing consumerism both have impacted the overall well-being of people. Everyone is running a race where they don't know who they are competing with and all this time the competition is with their own self.

There's a dire need to understand the consequences of instant gratification so that people can start moving towards lasting fulfilment. The technology platforms are good to use if they are used in moderation and for the purpose of accomplishing required work, but their overuse can result in stress and dissatisfaction. With increasing obsession for speed and need for instant results, people are harming their mental health and relationships. People need to get back to the foundations where patience was the key to fulfilled and content life. People need to learn and adopt patience in their lives, appreciate slow progress and growth, and at the same time prioritize physical and mental well-being.

People have fallen victims to an endless cycle of digital interactions. With constant need for checking emails, notifications, scrolling through the social media content and feeds, and taking part in online arguments, there develops an endless cycle of repetitive tasks. These activities often lack any meaningful outcomes thus causing dissatisfaction and futility. American Psychological Association conducted a study on the impact of social media on teenagers. The results of the study revealed that those who spend more than three hours a day on social media is more likely to suffer from some kind of mental health problems including depression and anxiety. Another survey conducted revealed that nearly half of Americans report feeling alone, left out or not understood. Digital connectivity is good till the time it's serving its purpose and the usage is limited to accomplish tasks only. Excessive usage can create an illusion of social interactions, virtual presence and influence, leading to isolation and loneliness.

Social media and online platforms not only cause a sense of left out, but are also causing addiction in the younger generations. A study conducted on online activity reported that 28 percent of adults are almost online that can contribute to addiction and reduced attention spans. Another study involving Norwegian individuals ranging from 16 to 88 years of age reported a more frequent association of anxiety with addiction to social media use. As per studies conducted globally, the findings also suggest that excessive use of social media networks can result in lower self-esteem. Adolescents are constantly online today and they are the most vulnerable among all, who feel dissatisfied and have a sense of being left-out after spending time online.

The digital age has also given rise to increased pursuit of material wealth. The digital platforms showcase different types of products and people using them. They also show extravagant lifestyles of people thus promoting the pursuit of material wealth. Advertising media is using the social media platforms and other applications for promoting their products. They create interesting and attractive narratives through ads on these platforms that the young people get attracted and then they start falling prey to the endless cycle of consumerism. In traditional times, people used to live a lifestyle based on principles and values. But in the modern world, people are pretty open in sharing their life with others, their lifestyle and the wealth they have accumulated. This gives them a sense of achievement and temporary pleasure. But when all of a sudden, they lose popularity, they become vulnerable and fall prey to depression. Those constantly watching such ads and lifestyles of others feel attracted and at the same time left out as they are not able to afford that. This again leads to sense of anxiety and depression.

People start questioning themselves by watching others on these social media platforms. The question often led to a sense of left behind or failure depending on the context. People have lost connection with themselves and others as well, with rising influence of social media. The virtual world has taken over completely and with more virtual environmental simulations under experimentation people would get more isolated going forward.

Ease of access to information is causing information overload for people and they are getting more confused with so much available with them. They often lose sight of the real problem at hand and get absorbed in all the other information thrown at them. Information age has created some form of equality in human beings where these platforms are accessible for everyone and the information lying there is free to access as well. People feel pressured to stay updated with latest trends and activities happening globally and this results in increased anxiety and stress. Every information is available at fingertips and thus people feel it less relevant that they learn and memorize important information. This is resulting in loss of memory power, as the more people have to store, the less they focus on the key information pieces.

An ancient Greek mythology story about Pandora, the first women who was given a box and was instructed not to open it. But Pandora had a sense of curiosity that led her to open the box. The box contained all the evils of the world including disease, death, violence, greed, and madness. As the box was opened, all the evils were released, leaving only hope inside the box. Pandora box symbolizes dangers of unchecked curiosity, unforeseen consequences and unleashing of challenges and struggles. The modern-day digital age with overwhelming digital information can be compared with Pandora box. The internet and digital age have opened up many opportunities, wide array of information and connectivity, but it has also unveiled host of challenges including misinformation, fake news, cyberbullying, gaming and digital addiction. So, it's important to understand the double-edged nature of curiosity and progress. To progress and navigate this digital landscape, people need to find balance between, set right expectations and right boundaries. This would involve practices such as digital detox, mindfulness, and staying away from the gadgets when there's no need. This will help reduce the negative effects of constant connectivity.

People are running an endless race and somewhere deep down they have started realizing this. This feeling of emptiness after chasing wealth endlessly forces them to search for meaning and purpose in life. They are in constant search for meaning and purpose in all their actions. In the world filled with so much of digital distractions, it's important to engage in activities that foster human relationships, personal growth and overall well-being of communities and societies. People need to practice gratitude to get rid of their sense of pursuit of material wealth and thankfully cherish what they already have. This age of information and connectedness is not completely bad or good, but it depends on how people engage with and use technology.

Hindu mythology has some good references in form of stories that can help get insight into the need for balance in this digital age. Karna was a warrior granted with divine Armor and earrings *(Kavach and Kundal)* for protection and these divine gifts provided him strength and virtue. But for seeking validation and acceptance, he gives them away to Indra with a hope for support and recognition. This single decision of Karna left him vulnerable in the battlefield of Kurukshetra and led to his fall. This story reveals that sense of validation and support can lead to vulnerability to mental health issues and emotional distress. Similarly, those seeking online validation are often vulnerable and develop anxiety, mental issues like depression.

The story of Ravana is another example of isolation and detachment. Ravana created a magnificent golden city, a symbol of extreme wealth and power. Despite having many allies and subjects, he remained isolated due to his ego and pride. Thus, he wasn't able to connect with others and form genuine relationships. His isolation and loss of moral values led to his defeat by Lord Rama. The isolation and detachment from the moral values and principles led to fall of Ravana. The digital world provides a false sense of connectedness all the time, but in reality, it's leading to more isolation from the physical world with loss of human relationships. The superficial online interactions may feel good in the beginning, but in the long run, lead to isolation, loneliness and disconnectedness.

The story of Narada, the heavenly sage who often spread rumours to test integrity of people. Once the rumour spread by Narada backfired and it created confusion and conflict among the gods. To restore peace and reveal the truth, divine intervention was required. This incident taught Narada a lesson about the ill and disastrous effects of misinformation. The digitally connected world is filled with many false rumours and misinformation. All these can lead to disastrous results in the society with widespread fear, anxiety, mistrust and societal harm.

There are references in our traditional texts and these references are a good source to learn about the right way of living in digital age. Having right balance by setting boundaries for usage of social media and other platforms is important to prevent the ill-effects of digital technologies. The stories from ancient texts tells us the importance of human relationships, discipline, moderation, and focus on long-term goals rather than seeking instant gratification. The digital age is filled with both benefits and challenges and it has the promise of prosperity and peril both. It's the responsibility of humans to navigate wisely, and see to it that they don't lose humanity in this progression.

Various important steps can be taken to establish healthy digital life:

- **Digital education**: Education is important for awareness and right usage. So, educating people on becoming more responsible in using digital platforms is paramount. People should be aware about how to verify the information and recognize the impact of misinformation on our lives, so that the spread of misinformation can be controlled.

- **More human interactions**: People should prioritize in-person interactions over digital ways of communication, as this can help counter the sense of isolation and strengthen societal bonds. Scheduling outdoor activities and spending time with near and dear ones can help strengthening the relationships.

- **Limits of usage**: Establishing clear boundaries for usage of digital media and platforms can limit the use and prevent overload and burnout. It's important to designate specific time for any digital activity such as email check, social media interactions, virtual learning etc.

- **Practice patience and mindfulness**: Digital era has brought down the attention span of people and they want instant gratification in everything. They need to practice patience and mindfulness to reduce stress and anxiety in life. There are many digital detox techniques that can be tried to boost control and patience. It's important to take breaks from the digital media time to time so that the overall span of usage is reduced and this in turn would reduce stress and anxiety.

♦ **Questioning the source of information**: With the widespread usage of digital platforms, there's load of misinformation on the online channels. So, critical thinking is required to question the source of information being provided online. Consideration is required to understand the motivation behind the misinformation, so that it can be tracked and stopped from further spread.

In summary, there's enormous potential in the digital era that can help with progress and innovation. But special consideration is required to create an ecosystem where right usage is promoted and propagated. People need to work together towards achieving the right usage and balance, which in turn would help in reducing stress and anxiety from life. There's need to embrace the lessons from the past and consider practical strategies that can be adopted to have a healthier digital life. Technology is a very good servant, but a terrible master that can lead humanity to destruction. So, it's important that we start taking steps and work towards the goal of creating balance and promote the right usage of digital technology.

Chapter 8

THE CONSUMER CULTURE – IS IT JEOPARDIZING THE FUTURE OF HUMANS?

Three best friends Vicky, Ajay and Arun who grew up together in the same town, shared very similar backgrounds but learnt different lessons in life based on their family situations. Families of all three had humble backgrounds and their spending habits and patterns were almost similar. But the three friends have very different approach to life when it comes to managing their finances, fulfilling their desires and living the life.

Vicky is a conservative person and believes in saving for any uncertain situations and future. He is a firm believer of the traditional idea that one should live below the means so that they can live life comfortably without stretching too much, as that leads to stress and anxiety in life. Vicky is very particular about his savings and investments. He is very calculative about his spending and restricts his budget and spends less on any desires that arise from social and peer pressure. He believes that **"financial security is more important over enjoying the momentary pleasures that material possessions give"**. When he needed a car for his family, he chose to focus on practicality and reliability and bought a reliable used car, for which he paid in cash. This saved him from the burden of any debt and monthly EMIs. It also left room for him to save more.

Vicky's home choices were also very prudent and he didn't believe in stretching his budget to buy a bigger, luxurious house which he could show off in the society. When he bought his house, he focused on limiting his debt exposure and bought a small comfortable apartment in a mid-rise residential society. Even his home furnishings reflected his practical nature as he chose limited and required furnishings for the house. This decision allowed him to save for future and could allow him to buy a bigger house if needed. He has very similar approach for other things as well. As an example, he buys technology when absolutely necessary and chose refurbished models that can meet his basic needs. Overall, he was pretty clear about saving and investing for future and living a comfortable life by serving his present day needs well.

Fast forward few years, Vicky's saving and investing discipline paid off. His savings and investments grew significantly, providing him the required funds for covering any emergencies, pay for his modest living expenses and have a good portfolio for retirement. Once retired, he could enjoy his life and provide for his family through these savings and investments. Vicky lived his life with peace of mind and his belief in attaining financial security paid off.

Ajay is a moderate spender and tries to enjoy comforts and luxuries of life in moderation. He has a balanced approach towards life. He creates budget for everything he buys and saves a portion of his earnings for the future. He occasionally indulges into satisfying his desires. He enjoys the pleasure of modern life within reasonable limits. His budgeting includes a portion of income that he can use for occasional indulgences. While buying a car, Ajay considered a mid-variant of a new car that provided him good value for money. After making the purchase, he kept the car for many years to ensure that he doesn't have to make big purchase again for years to come. His house buying decision also involved a sense of moderation, when he purchased a reasonably priced house in good locality with moderate mortgage which he could easily manage and thus create a balance in life. He also ensured good furnishings at moderate prices that made his house look good. His approach to gadgets was of similar mindset as well. He used to upgrade technology occasionally, especially at times when the old technology becomes outdated.

Fast forward few years, Ajay's life was filled with a comfortable lifestyle without much financial pressure and moderate security and savings for retirement. He enjoyed all aspects of life and indulgences without going too much out of the pocket. He ensured decent savings so that he didn't have to worry about his and his family's expenses and any emergency situations. His approach towards life and finances allowed him to have a balanced life with a sense of security and comfort.

Arun is different from the other two. He believes in having the finest things in life and often ends up spending more than his income. He is focused on prioritizing status, luxury and comfort in life as he believes that these things represent one's success. When Arun bought a car, he went for the top end of the luxury model financed with a high rate of interest. He also got into the habit of frequently upgrading his car within just 3-5 years of use. This habit led him into the financial burden.

His house buying decision was also based on social, peer pressure and he sought acknowledgement and complement for his purchases from his friends, family and relatives. He liked living an extravagant lifestyle and this led to many financial difficulties in his life. After buying house, he purchased high quality expensive furnishings and did extra interior work to make house look good and lavish. He used to buy the latest expensive gadgets on credit and replaced them frequently with the new one's again through debt. He wanted to stay ahead of the trends in the market.

Fast forward few years, his lifestyle led him into financial mess. He had accumulated substantial debt and was struggling with making loan payments, this led to further financial stress and impacted the overall well-being and quality of life. Even though he had a luxurious home, modern gadgets and luxurious shiny car, he found little peace in life and he was constantly stressed with his finances. His pursuit of material possessions and wealth left him vulnerable to economic downturns and personal financial crisis. He wasn't able to retire comfortably and was forced to work beyond the retirement age just to serve the mounting debt.

As we witnessed from the above story that different choices made by friends led to distinct outcomes. Vicky's simplistic lifestyle and focused savings helped him enjoy his stress-free life and plan better for a comfortable retirement. He was able to enjoy simple pleasures of life without indulging too much into peer-pressure, acknowledgement, social status. He felt happy the way he spent his life. He maintained a balanced lifestyle with less worries and stress in the workplace as well. He never forced himself to work extra time under pressure, as he planned his financial security and freedom better. Ajay's balanced approach helped him enjoy the life alongside enjoy material possessions as well. He was able to lead a comfortable, stable life with enough room for enjoyment and future planning. He used to find satisfaction in his small achievements and maintained a healthy financial status. But Arun's extravagant lifestyle pushed him into debt crisis which led him feel stretched all the time at workplace and even work extra beyond the normal retirement age. He wasn't able to save much due to his expenses on expensive material possessions which didn't matter much after a few days or weeks of use. His focus on constantly chasing material possessions left him exhausted and dissatisfied with life.

The above story reflects relatable situations from the modern world where people often stretch on their finances to acquire that extra material possession which hardly add any real value to their lives. Consumer culture has become dominant in the today's society, that's impacting individuals, social values and economic principles and practices. This is not a **"just now"** thing which has cropped up suddenly, it has taken years of evolutionary challenges and **"changed mindset"** of being inclined towards material wealth and possession. This is driven by a combination of historical, social, economic, and technological factors. Going back to industrialization era, tells us that the seeds of consumer culture were sown there. Industrialization brought in techniques of mass production of goods at significant pace and scale, which led to wider availability of these products. This transition established the foundation of consumer-culture and consumer-oriented society.

Post world-war II period further accelerated the growth of consumer-culture. Increased disposable incomes of people, rise of urban living, led to the surge in demand for variety of consumer goods including automobiles, household appliances, entertainment devices and much more. Then the companies started advertising their products to increase sales and earn profits, which further supported the growth of consumption. Soon the companies started linking their products with national prosperity and national dreams that further propelled the consumerism. In the modern world, people often consider consumer goods as a symbol of their status and personal identity. People connect and have obsession about brands as if these products are the only important ingredient in their lives. The fashion industry, luxury goods are some examples that pushed the linkage between personal identity and the goods. People use brands to express their individuality, status and lifestyle.

Modern societies have significant contribution in fuelling consumer culture through comparison and measuring the worth of individuals against the material possessions held by them. The advent of social media and other technology platforms added fuel to the fire where people started displaying their possessions, lifestyle, and wealth that created pressure to conform to certain living and consumption standards. Economy became the focal point with capitalism promoting the consumer culture with emphasis on continuous growth and further evolution. Businesses are worried about their sale of products; profits earned and produce more to reach out to more consumers. Innovation and new products have become the priority of businesses to drive sales and earn more profits. This **endless cycle of production and consumption** is the central hook essential for the functioning of modern world, where acquiring material wealth is the sole objective.

Connected global ecosystem i.e., "Globalization" allowed people to connect and compare their material possessions, new products they can acquire and much more. This expanded the consumerism and provided businesses with platform to produce and earn more. The goods started becoming accessible globally that further triggered the demand for expensive, luxurious products thus leading to more production. Logistics and global supply chain companies supported by ensuring that products can be produced economically in one region and sold at higher prices in the other region. The connected global marketplace today is a great example of growth of consumerism. E-commerce companies with their platforms has gotten closer to the people (**so called customers**) offering them variety of product choices to choose from. Everything is getting accessible and available at a simple click of button. Technology is helping corporations to read human behaviour, their buying patterns, their emotional inclinations and much more. This is further helping the corporations to do targeted marketing and promotion of their products to drive sales by stimulating consumer desires.

When the first material desire arose in the mind of human beings, it was based on the quest for means that can help design a secure and comfortable life. The sense of security was achieved when humans learnt how to fulfil their basic needs of food, water, shelter and clothes. Once the mind was satisfied with security, then it gave rise to another desire of searching beyond the needs. The journey of desire started from there. A certain group of people further started thinking in the direction that how they can start establishing control over the masses and they started working towards searching, discovering and inventing new things, products, articles or materials based on people's desires. It was a **consensus to embark on this journey of consumerism,** as nothing appeared too much in the beginning and people looked at all the discoveries as means to add more comfort to their lives. This consensus further accelerated the pace of production of goods and services leading to growing consumerism. The journey started then, is still continuing and today the situation is such that there are not few groups or individuals who are a part of this journey, instead everyone has become a participant in it. Modern world is filled with the materials produced by the humans, for the humans and to accumulate more wealth for the future. Cities are today crowded with so many people that it has become really difficult to survive in cities if people don't have enough earnings. This is the trigger that's forcing people to get into hectic jobs where they spend their days and nights to earn more and cover up for a lifestyle which is like a mirage in the desert. The unending quest has begun and people have lost the sense of satisfaction and fulfilment. There are very few who still care and bother about the natural habitats and ecosystem. Cities has lost connection to nature and this is causing lot of destruction around the world.

"Where are humans leading themselves?", is a critical question to ask and ponder. The sense of security and safety is a natural instinct that needs addressal, but going beyond that and running an endless race where there are no destinations and just chase for an illusionary success, isn't worth it. Humans are intelligent, emotional and spiritual beings, but today they have lost all these basic traits and are becoming merely part of a journey which in itself is not worth taking. Humans have used their own psychological behaviour to create subjects and studies, which now they are using to manipulate each other and become a customer of disaster. Corporations have their own mandates so they can't stop thinking about wealth creation and profits. But people need to give it a serious thought that what they are really becoming and would it be good for the coming generations to pursue the same journey. There's a need for coarse correction and collective effort to choose the right direction that can bring in harmony, peace, contentment and fulfilment in people's lives.

Having all this discussion now is important as it's better to be late than never. People are becoming overly dependent and have become slaves to their senses and desires. The rational thinking has taken a back seat and all this is driven by them only, as there are corporations, businesses, governments, institutions and many other groups and communities who continue to drive consumerism. The single central idea is economy. How will economy run if people don't transact, purchase and consume all that which is being produced. But a bigger question is – **"Why is it all required?"** There's a larger economy which is calling humans today to save it and that's the economy of nature. Nature has provided humans with almost everything that's essential for survival. But they didn't stop there and continued the chase of their desires. They continue to do so today and will continue in the future as well if there's no alarm to get into a consensus that there's a need for serious introspection and coming to an agreement that how and what is the right thing to do.

As we presented a story of three friends in the beginning of the chapter, there are some interesting lessons to learn from the lives of these friends.

First lesson is that – one should strive to create a life that follows a well-balanced approach between enjoying life's pleasures and maintaining financial stability and security. This approach helps avoid any extreme situations in life such as huge debt with inability to clear it off. One should focus on attaining financial security and continue to enjoy life by fulfilling material desires as per one's income limit.

Second lesson is – if possible, try to live below the means and create a better and secure future. Living below the means doesn't mean that one shouldn't spend at all, rather there should be prioritization of needs over desires. If the needs are fulfilled and there's ample amount of savings for short and long-term goals, then one should fulfil desires with the surplus within limits. Sometimes, there are instances when one needs to deliberately avoid big expenses to cover up for the more important expenses and save for the future financial security.

Third lesson is – prioritize happiness, security, fulfilment, and peace of mind over material wealth and avoid the race of consumerism. True fulfilment never comes from satisfying material desires. Material desires are like mirage, they keep on moving with every milestone achieved and this means that it's an endless race one should avoid. True fulfilment and security come by prioritizing human relations and experiences over material things.

If humans start focusing on the economy of nature, they would be much better off and the real evolution would help the planet to prosper in the right way. The pursuit of material wealth has blinded the humans and consumer-driven lifestyle has taken over. In all this chase, humans often overlook the simplicity and abundance provided by the economy of nature. The artificial economy created for wealth accumulation hasn't much to offer to all human beings with equality, whereas nature's economy offers resources that are freely available to everyone, thus creating a sense of equality and harmony among people. The clean air for breathing, the fresh and clean water for drinking and fertile soil for producing food are freely available for everyone and nature doesn't restrict any of its resources. These resources are the most important ones for survival of human beings. For material pursuits, humans have taken these resources for granted. If humans start prioritizing the conservation of these resources over their chase for material wealth, the planet would become a heavenly abode for everyone. This neglected work is far more important in the modern times as the pace of exploitation of these resources have significantly increased with the advent of industrialization, technology, digital and the process goes on. The talks of sustainability and environmental protection are taken up in such a way as if environment and resources are meant to be exploited and there's no need to conserve anything.

"What aligns with nature's economy?" Common land pool, community gardens can significantly transform the urban areas into beautiful green landscapes, alongside providing fresh organic product for the society. These common spaces and land, support in developing a sense of community and shared purpose. With common areas and land, people can work together and share knowledge and ideas with each other. This strengthens the relationships and overall wellbeing of society. Initiatives such as use of renewable energy sources, solar and wind power help to reduce the reliance on fossil fuels that can help reduce pollution and mitigate extremities due to climate change. All this aligns with nature's economy, that can promote healthy relationships, societal bonds, overall wellbeing and balance in the communities, societies and countries. The only need is to understand that establishing the ecological balance is much more important than the short-term growth and gain.

Bhutan is a good example of the society that values natural economy over the material wealth. Bhutan, a small Himalayan kingdom, measures the progress of region through Gross National Happiness (GNH) instead of Gross Domestic Product (GDP). The commitment of this region highlights a holistic approach towards development and growth, where wellbeing of people, environmental conservation are prioritized to achieve sustainable growth. Bhutan has mandated that at least 60% of the country must remain forests. The country has also achieved carbon neutrality and prefer renewable energy (hydropower) to meet the energy needs. Bhutan's holistic approach provides an important framework for overall development, growth and collective well-being by embracing nature's economy. The example of Bhutan shows that how is it possible to progress and prosper without damaging the environment and well-being of people.

Living in nature has long lasting impact on happiness, physical and mental wellbeing. It helps reduce stress, improves the emotional wellbeing and enhances overall cognitive function. Activities done in natural environment such as hiking, walking in green park/ garden helps creating a connection with nature and provides a sense of peace which is missing the modern-day life. In essence, there are numerous benefits of living and immersing in natural environment. The only need is the shift of focus from material possessions to conservation and appreciation of natural resources. In this way, it's possible to create a society that values well-being, collective harmony over material wealth. The shift is not easy, as it would require tremendous effort in shift of mindset, values and priorities. But once done, the benefits are immense. Humans can learn to recreate the connection with nature, build a more equitable, fit and peaceful society. This will help the future generations immensely and they will thank their older generations for the beautiful gift they would get.

Chapter 9

MENTAL STATE OF AFFAIRS — WHY SO MUCH ANXIETY AND FEAR?

It's a bright day with birds and animals busy with their daily chores of searching and collecting food. Somewhere near the river, there are caves holding predators who are resting with their stomach full. The forest is silent till these predators' rest, as once they wake up and go on hunt, the whole silence would fill up with fear and anxiety. Hidden in some ancient structures erected upon steep rocks, are few humans who are challenged by the predatory environment and the struggle for survival is evident in their fear and anxiety. Some days would pass by without any attempt to get down into the forest land, as predators are roaming to satisfy their hunger. There have been many encounters with predators in the past and this will continue in future as well, till humans learn to protect themselves from the predatory environment and create some security and safety for themselves. The key emotions are fear and anxiety of survival. There are more humans around, but all are separated by scarcity of space at one place. They are distributed and thus weak in planning, hunting and ensuring their survival. The first hurdle for everyone is to protect themselves, feed their hunger and sleep comfortably without any fear.

Early man's life was not an easy affair to handle. The level of stress, fear and anxiety were tremendous, but the instinct to protect and survive was far stronger. Years of struggle and living a life filled with fear, humans learnt a lot of things such as – making tools for protection and hunting, burning leaves and woods for fire, making small compartments with woods that are strong enough to protect them from attacks and harsh weather conditions. The learning process was slow and it took many decades to overcome the fear of survival and add security and safety to life. But once the initial learning happened, it was followed by fast progress. As centuries went by, humas evolved and started living in societies, communities, regions, tribes. There were better tools with them along with skillset they learnt during the years of evolution. These tools and skillset helped humans to formulate the societies with required materials, structures and other required necessities. Agriculture was the turning point in the lives of humans, as they were now able to settle and give up their nomadic life. They were now able to settle at one place, grow their own food, and create their own stable structures called homes. This stability allowed them to control their closed environment and minimize the threat of predatory environment. So, the humans' life eased out with this transition and they were able to focus on other things such as forming organized societies and all this marked significant shift in their emotions.

The transition in mental state and emotions was significant. The emotions of anxiety and fear were now layered over by security, safety and stability. The worries of being hunted by predators faded away and this gradually gave way to the sense of security and confidence. There was ample time to focus on the planning, building communities, cultivating lands, and laying down the foundation of societies, communities and tribes. Humans started to establish trade with other communities and tribes. This further marked the progress and now they were in a better position to take charge of natural resources. They started domesticating animals, constructed their homes, developed new techniques to do farming. The new emotions took over and these were pride, ambition and desire for more. These emotions further triggered another phase of struggle for humans. The previous emotions of fear and anxiety were now transformed into a continuous quest for control and dominance.

The rising greed gave rise to conflicts and wars between the communities and tribes. They fought over resources, land and power causing widespread destruction and suffering. The ambitions and aspirations led to desire of expansion of wealth and influence. This new quest for control and dominance gave rise to a new form of fear and anxiety. These new feelings were now related to the wealth and material possessions. There was a fear and continuous anxiety of losing material possessions and wealth which humans had gained so far.

History has so many stories that reflect on the fact that the growing greed of humans always led to destruction. Some of the lessons from the Hindu scripture Mahabharata highlights the destructive power of greed. The story of Mahabharata revolves around the rise of entire Kuru dynasty, followed by the rivalry between the Kauravas and Pandavas. The five Pandavas brothers, and their hundred cousins led by Duryodhana entered into a war for the throne of Hastinapur, and this war led to huge destruction for both the sides. Duryodhana was jealous of his Pandavas cousins all his life, as he was completely blinded by his greed and desire for taking over the entire dynasty. From his childhood, he was envious of his cousins because of their virtues and popularity, especially Arjuna. Pandavas was having every right to be the real heir to the throne after the demise of their father, King Pandu. In the interim, Dhritarashtra was given the control to look after the kingdom, till the Pandavas reach their adolescent. But Dhritarashtra got blinded by his ambition and desire to be the king and make his eldest son Duryodhana be the successor after him. His ambition and desire worked as poison for his son who started envying his cousins. These emotions of greed, ambition, jealousy and hate laid the foundation of whole conflict of Mahabharata.

The greed and ambition led to the disastrous war of Kurukshetra, where both the sides suffered heavy losses. Many legendary warriors, leaders and numerous soldiers lost their lives in the battle. The result of this war was a landscape of death and desolation, reflecting the futility and destructive nature of greed and selfish desire.

The winning side of Pandavas were also left with huge losses, and they too grappled with deep sorrow and emptiness after the war. This whole epic offers a great deal of learning for the generations to come, especially on the warnings against the dangers of greed and the importance of accepting the righteousness. The story of Mahabharata also highlights the fact that how the desire for power and control can corrupt the individuals and lead to their downfall. It emphasizes the value of morality, self-restraint and integrity.

It might appear that humans are able to overcome the fear and anxiety around survival, but these emotions haven't completely disappeared, instead they have changed their focus and realm. As humans started focusing on chasing and accumulating the material wealth and power, a new emotion of greed started taking over. The endless desire for more took the front seat and became the key driver for further evolution and progress. Humans desired more land, more resources, more power, more control and more influence and this whole process of wanting more led to the development of social hierarchies and class systems, where one class started dominating over the others and the gap between the rich and poor started widening. This class and societal division brought in more conflicts and wars. People started fighting over resources, territories, regions, and power causing destruction and disaster.

Looking at the today's era, the modern world – the emotions of fear and anxiety still exist, but they exist in different form. Today humans are not worried about their security from predators, nor they have that endless struggle of finding food for survival. But today they have gathered a lot of material possessions and wealth and the fear and anxiety are linked to the loss and maintenance of these material possessions and wealth. So, in essence, the modern humans are still plagued by the same feeling as their predecessors, but the difference is that the fear is no more for life and survival, but for the possessions which they have gathered by working so hard.

Looking closely into the lives of successful people flashes up the reality. Successful people *(as per modern world's definition people who have enormous material wealth and possessions and they earn handsomely well)* living in big metropolitan cities, having good jobs, beautiful and luxurious houses and having all the comfort and luxury that money can purchase, are still constantly worried and anxious about their future. There's a deep fear of financial instability, continuous pressure to maintain the current lifestyle of luxury and comfort. The unending chase of material pursuit and social validation has led to a culture of comparison and competition. The modern tools and technologies further aggravate the problem. People strive to present their best and perfect image on social media platforms to seek for social validation and praise. This continuous pressure leads to the feeling of inadequacy, unfulfillment and dissatisfaction.

Modern humans have a common story where fear and anxiety are part of lives similar to their ancestors. The only difference is that today they are striving for more and more. The basic survival is achieved for most, but there's **social survival which has become the new normal** and that's the cause of deep-rooted anxiety in the societies. As we look at the journey from early man to modern era, it's pretty clear that the feelings of anxiety and fear has remained constant. There's just a shift in focus from maintaining survival to accumulating and maintaining material possessions and wealth. Today, the mental state of humans is even worse as there are more avenues and so is the relentless pursuit.

When we look into the mental state of affairs and delve deeper into the psychological and emotional consequences of material pursuits, it becomes pretty evident that modern societies are living under significant pressure, which is further amplified by the digital technology and social media. This in result is causing widespread mental health issues, loss of human relations, and a deep sense of dissatisfaction. With consumerism culture, there's push for acquiring more and this endless pursuit keep humans continuously under stress. It also strains the natural resources. Humans are stuck in this endless loop of evolutionary and societal pressures causing all the issues. These issues are not only causing mental problems, but also affecting the overall health and well-being of the society as a whole.

The modern era is witnessing significant rise in the mental health cases, where people have fallen victims to this loop of materialism. They are aspiring for more artificial economy and the whole artificial economy thrives on the insecurities of humans. There's need to embrace practices that can help prioritize mental and emotional well-being over material possessions and pursuits. Practices such as mindfulness, nature therapy, slow movement etc., are among few that can help find balance and fulfilment.

Amidst of this anxiety and fear, there's an interesting aspect of humans that is the **illusion of control**. Modern era with all its technological advancements and material wealth offers a false impression to humans that they have mastered the environment. Humans have done so much with natural resources that now there's a sense of control inside their mind. This control is just an illusion stemming from the roots of material pursuits. From making smaller structures, to big ones, roads, bridges, railway tracks, buildings, compartments, planes, buses, ships and all that so called infrastructure to support the dreams of comfort and luxuries, humans have got the deep-rooted belief that they have established control on the natural resources and they can keep on doing this for rest of their existence. But when the reality hits illusion, there's a disaster awaiting to impede the false hopes and false sense of security, control and stability. There's no doubt in it that humans have manipulated the surroundings, are able to predict the weather conditions, and even make alterations to the biological existence to some extent. But with all these achievements, the deep sense of fear and anxiety still persists. This is further heightened by the very technology and tools designed to alleviate them.

Look around and you can see people struggling with all the products and services they are using. There are so many industries, factories, companies, closed institutions, smaller units and almost everyone is engaged and involved in creating some form of product or service. All these products and services are being created to transact with others. Those who are using these products and services are becoming used to the comfort being added to their lives through their use. But with all this added comfort and convenience, there's an added sense of anxiety added along with it. The anxiety of losing this added comfort and convenience. When a product or service goes out of order for some time, the added comfort is lost and thus adds stress to people's life. There's so much dependence being created in each and every walk of life that all this comfort is not adding anymore comfort, but instead alleviating the sense of anxiety and fear in humans. But the problem at hand is even bigger than this. **The habit of wanting more and longing for even more is becoming a common menace for humans**. If this menace is not checked in the near term, then in the long term this will be disastrous to the planet.

Planet is already struggling and the struggle is further alleviated every single day by the growing activity of humans. They are continuously looking to create more products for their comfort and convenience and for this purpose they are exploiting the natural resources. More factories to boost production is causing harm to clean air which is the basic need for the humans to survive on this planet. More roads and railway tracks to connect each and every corner in the country and world so that people can roam around quickly, they can reach from one place to another faster and they save more time. More buildings, apartments, closed structures built over the land by cutting more forests. The growing deforestation is a concern for the planet as this is destroying the ecological balance of nature and causing more destruction everywhere and the nominee to this destruction is not only humans, but also other species who are part of this planet. All this is named as development and evolution by humans and they are continuously cherishing their developments and taking pride in establishing this control. But when reality crosses their path, even then they hardly realize that they have got it all wrong. All these so-called achievements that humans have gathered so far, are adding more fear and anxiety to their lives.

Humans believe and behave in a way that natural resources are abundant and they can keep on exploiting them till their existence. But they are badly mistaken in their judgment and the result of this is the global destruction and aftermath originating from all the success and achievements of humans. To establish a sense of control and accelerate the pace of accumulation of material possessions, humans are continuously making and producing more. In the modern era, the corporations who are entitled to produce goods for public use are taking advantage of their position and entitlement by making products that have a limited lifespan, a lifespan which is even shorter to the extent that those buying and using it would have to keep on buying it very frequently. For those who are making these reliable products are forced to keep on innovating and releasing newer versions of it so that they can attract people to upgrade and buy the new products and keep the revenues flowing into the company. This reflects that there's a constant sense of staying relevant and updated with the trends that's keeping humans trapped in a never-ending loop of consumption, dissatisfaction and unfulfillment.

Going back in the era, early humans were pretty much focused on ensuring their survival and thus their prime objective was to fulfil their basic needs. They had limited choices and the decision making was pretty straightforward which encompassed needs such as – finding food, shelter, get rid of danger. The simplistic choices though part of their necessities ultimately led them to a less anxious and confusion free life. Their life was filled with simplicity and was based on natural principle of **"less is more"**. This is relevant in the modern world and for the modern humans too, who can start making their lives simplistic, less focused on too much clutter and embrace peace and clarity over confusion and ambiguity.

There are lot of ancient practices which are very relevant for modern humans and these practices can really help clearing a lot of anxiety and stress from their lives. Ancient spiritual traditions where mindfulness and meditation were the key practices for managing stress and anxiety, help humans to focus on the present and live their life in the present moment by adopting a sense of awareness and acceptance. Humans have the differentiation from other living beings through their intelligence and emotions. With this differentiation comes an equally important task of controlling and managing the emotions through continuous observation and live in the present moment. Human desires that have resulted in the luxuries and material prosperity of the modern world has all come from the initial emotions and thoughts of humans. The uncontrolled desires resulted into the destruction of the ecological balance of natural environment. Today, the condition of modern man is no different than someone isolated in the middle of a huge ocean with no idea of way out. Ancient practices of mindfulness and mediation focus on controlling one's mind and bring it to a point where the practitioner becomes the observer and no longer remains the doer. This observer knows everything and still doesn't take part in doing or achieving anything, as there's no engagement, involvement or indulgence.

The art of mindfulness teaches humans a lot about their existence and the existence of nature. The two need to stay in harmony and this is the real meaning of existence. Human evolution and transformation that has happened so far is pretty focused on the instincts and desires that originated from human thoughts and they took action to convert these desires into reality and that's what the world is a manifestation of. Humans are pretty aware of the fact that what happens when unchecked desires transform into reality. The reality coexists with increasing fear and anxiety and the result is a chaos that's ever transmitting. Buddha, Mahavira, Swami Vivekananda and many more ancient masters delivered to the world the most important practice of meditation and mindfulness. The practices were delivered with an inclusive approach which means that everyone tried to deliver their practice keeping into consideration their relevance in the real world. None mentioned that humans should stop the progression and journey on which they are already headed onto. But they have one thing in common in their practices and preachings – **"Need for balance"**. Humans need to have a balanced approach to survive and suffice on this planet. Extremities won't ever result into a harmonious life on this planet.

What's the real path to a sustainable living?

Sustainable living demands and emphasizes on a lifestyle that promotes harmony with nature and minimum environmental impact. This approach requires significant amount of effort to make conscious decisions about the consumption of resources and waste generation. By following the sustainable living approach, humans can establish a balance with nature and recreate the balance that's lost thus far. This will further help in establishing the well-being of all beings and the whole planet. Some of the initiatives already existing in the modern world includes – reducing the use of plastic, water conservation, adoption of renewable energy sources, and accelerating support for more local and organic food production. The art of sustainable living would also help humans shift their focus away from the material pursuits towards relationships, physical and mental health.

Let's understand this whole concept through a short story. Once upon a time there lived a poor fisherman. He used to go catch fishes for serving his family's needs. One day, a magic golden fish was caught by him and this magic fish promised him to grant all his wishes if he releases her. Fisherman was a very kind and simple person and he simply released the golden fish into the sea. When he went back to his family, he told the whole incident to his wife. After hearing this, his wife sent him back to the sea to get a wish granted and to her surprise the wish was granted by the fish. After the first wish was granted, the fisherman's wife became greedy and now she wanted more – a new house, rather a palace, to become a noble lady, and become the Queen of land. All her wishes were granted by the fish. Once all her other wishes were fulfilled, now she wanted to be the Queen of land and sea both, and make golden fish to be her servant. When the fisherman went to the shore and talked about the new wish of his wife, the golden fish disappeared without a word. Fisherman returned back to his home. When he reached back, he saw his old mud hut, his poor old wife, and the broken stuff in the old condition.

The story has a powerful underlying message that resonates well with the condition of modern humans who are trapped in the endless pursuit of material wealth. This endless chase would ultimately lead to more desires and more desires would lead into dissatisfaction and emptiness. Humans have moved away from simple pleasures of life and they are in relentless race of accumulation that's causing constant discontentment. Humans need to remind themselves that life's meaning and true contentment is in appreciating the gift of nature and establishing a life that's in harmony with nature.

The fast-paced modern era is witness to alarming levels of depression among all age-groups. There's progression and advancement in all fields including technology, medicine, education, psychological and physical behaviour. Despite all this progression and advancements, the mental health issues continue to grow beyond the manageable levels. This clearly highlights the growing disconnect between material progression, advancements and emotional and mental well-being. Humans are finding themselves trapped in a vicious cycle of high expectations, competition, sustainability among the fast-growing urban culture, leading to growing stress, anxiety and sense of unfulfillment. With all this growth and evolution, humans have placed themselves in a spot where they are facing existential crisis, finding it difficult to answer the difficult questions of meaning and purpose of life.

Technology, social media and global connectivity have given rise to continuous comparison between the lives of people. People compare their lives with those of others and they start developing a feeling of jealousy and incompleteness. Social media platforms like Instagram and Facebook highlight the curated lives of people, showcasing the illusion of perfect living which appears unattainable. Those watching these curated versions of life develop the feelings of enviousness and low self-esteem. Those creating such fake glimpses and those watching them both misses out the whole point of meaning and purpose of doing all this. People keep on chasing the material possessions and wealth to fill their lives, but even after fulfilling their material goals, they feel unfulfilled with a lost sense of meaning and purpose in life.

Parents, who should be taking the hard ideal roles in life are also burdened with societal pressures. They often fall victim to the growing societal pressure and pass on this pressure to their children. From early on, parents instil in their children the sense of competition. From young age, children start competing with each other following the pressure of parents, teachers and the society. Academic success, extracurricular achievements, and future career prospects create so much pressure in the lives of children that they start becoming anxious from their very early days, losing the real charm and liveliness of childhood. They start developing the sense of insecurity, comparison, fear and stress from their childhood days. With their growing age, these feelings and emotions also grow and they keep shaping up increasing pressure on children. Children grow up in the society with a feeling that their real worth is measured by their academic success and achievements, not their own internal qualities. This further transforms the whole society and the cycle keeps on repeating till generations.

Competitiveness is a desire that's affecting individuals who want to distinguish, differentiate and surpass others. Nations compete with each other on various parameters such as economy, innovation, production, defence and much more. The competition among nations often lead to increased fear of losing out to each other, this sometimes led into conflicts and in worse cases result into military confrontations. The growing tensions between the nations trickles down to individual level, causing fear and uncertainty. When conflicts between nations escalate, there's a constant fear in people around their safety, security and the future. These nation level conflicts are extension of individual aspirations and desires. The quest for more and dominance over each other results into collective anxiety and unrest.

There's an unending search for something and that something is unknown,

An old journey that started long ago, fruits of thoughts, desires and
actions have grown,

Desires keep on igniting endless fires, actions help with navigation
and make the way,

Outcomes are unknown and mysterious, like long shadows of the day.

From the survival and basic needs, we set out on a path so wide,

To wander aimlessly, with no purpose and meaning set aside,

An unending loop of pursuits of illusion, where meaning
keeps fading away,

There's an endless chase for more, with a life that's lost the true ray.

Once afraid of predators and storms, now fear is a subtle thread,

Passing through our daily lives, from rising till bed,

There's continuous anxiety and restlessness, gathered possessions
don't appease,

An unending longing in hearts and minds, the needs that never sees.

Built great towers, conquered great lands and sailed across the
world through seas,

With a deep sense of emptiness still carried by the breeze,

In this quest for possessions and power, life's secret key is lost somewhere,

There's just chaos and destruction that we created around everywhere.

Let's pause a bit, stay calm for a while and listen to the inner call,

The peaceful whispers of the nature, the big rivers as they fall,

The nature holds in its arms, the answers of life,

The unending chase can cease, and true fulfilment will arise.

The journey pauses a bit, but not ends here,

Accept the now, this moment, however big or small, the new journey starts from here,

Try to find the balance with existence and be always free,

There's hidden purpose, that's an unknown now, you will be able to see...

Chapter 10

WEAPON OF SUSTAINABILITY – A MERE SHOW-OFF OR THE REAL KEY TO UNLOCK MORE LIFE?

Life is precious and it's true for every living being breathing on the planet. When it comes to living and right to live, every single being has an equal right and freedom. Today, in the modern world **"Sustainability" has become the new buzz-word**, as if it's an innovation which humans are discussing and working towards day-in day-out. Everyone in position of power, those running large corporations, heads of state and countries are talking about sustainability. Look around and see humans echoing big slogans and putting banners of **"Go-Green", "eco-friendly", "save the planet", "save mother nature"** and much more. All this eco and voices are fine, but there's a dire need to ask the real question that's crucial for humans – **"Is sustainability an option or innovation that needs to be a part of show-off or trend, or is it something that holds the key to future of this planet and thus the humanity and other beings' survival as well?"**

When so much is being spoken by individuals, it's very much required to be seen that what exactly the reality holds in store. World around is grappling with challenges that's threatening the sustainability of life. Everyone talks a lot about sustainability, but hardly someone comes forward to take the lead and command by setting an example for others to follow. Some very basic things that should be done are missing. Deforestation is increasing, issue of pollution is escalating at an accelerated pace, use of non-renewable fuel and resources is causing their extinction, and many such more issues are there in front of humans that demand an immediate addressal. **"How much action is really happening on the ground to mitigate the risks posed by these challenges?"** – that's something worth asking, but who would take the responsibility to ask and who would be answering it. Every single individual holds an equal accountability and should feel equally responsible to be a part of the change.

A story from ancient times shares the wisdom of living in harmony with nature. Cherokee, situated somewhere in the heart of what is now the southeastern United States, was known for living in harmony with nature. People of Cherokee were very particular about following the rhythms of seasons and the cycles of life, as they knew that their survival is dependent on the mother nature and surrounding environment. So, they always took good care of their surrounding environment. They believed in taking from nature as per their need and giving back to the land as well to ensure that it remains fertile and there's abundance for the coming generations as well.

One of the small Cherokee villages had tradition of planting the "Three Sisters: corn, beans, and squash". This companion plantation method was not just a technique, but it was a symbol of cooperation and balance. The beans enriched the soil with essential nitrogen, the squash spread out to cover the ground and the corn provided natural pole for the beans to climb. Squash also helped supressing weeds and retaining the required moisture necessary for the growth of plant. Once a boy saw his grandmother planting the seeds. Out of curiosity, he asked that why these three seeds are planted together. The grandmother smiled and answered that these seeds teach us a very important lesson – the lesson of **balance, support and harmony,** as they support each other in growing and spreading over the soil. Similarly, we humans should also live in harmony, with a balance in lives and support each other and work together for the betterment of everyone. Planting these three seeds together ensures that they thrive and ensure that the land remains good for the coming generations as well.

As time passed, the young boy saw wisdom in his grandmother's words. The Three Sisters flourished, and provided food for the village. This example of harmony with nature symbolizes that if people can learn to sustain themselves without depleting the natural resources, this planet would become a heavenly place to survive and thrive. Children when given such wisdom learns the important lessons of maintaining harmony with nature and they learn the essential lessons of sustainability and survival. Learning to have deep respect for land can teach children the lessons of true prosperity and the source of this prosperity is in staying in harmony with the nature.

There are many such lessons from the past which have hidden learnings that can help us make this world a better place. Going back to the past, when humans lived in a world where sustainability was not a choice, but a necessity. There was no luxury of disposable products, no comfort and convenience of other fashionable products. People relied on the practices that ensured not only their survival, but also the health of their surrounding environment. The traditional farming communities worked on the principles of sustainability. Farmers used to practice crop rotation, leave the land without any crop for some-time for resting and regenerating, use natural fertilizers to ensure soil health. All these practices ensured that the land remained fertile for future generations. Fast forward today and compare it with the modern farming, where new practices are depleting the essential soil nutrients that heavily rely on chemical fertilizers and pesticides, causing long term damage to soil and environment.

Modern humans are not just destroying the fertility of soil, they are in process of destroying their future generations too. Today, people are just worried about more. More crops, more consumption, more money, more power and more everything. It appears as if people are living for just accumulation and consumption. They hardly care if the value and quality of life is getting deteriorated day by day. Today, in the urban areas, people are eating the worst foods filled with poisonous substances like pesticides, chemical fertilizers etc. None of these substances provide any nutrition to humans, instead they destroy their health. But none is worried about this worst state of affairs around. Everyone is just aspiring for profits. Farmers are interested in growing and producing more crop so that they can sell more. For that they hardly think twice before using extra fertilizers and keep on putting more and more with every passing season. The soil keeps on losing nutrients and fertility and after sometime it become completely unfertile causing long lasting damage and permanent loss. None is worried about the long-lasting impact of the practices being followed, but instead people are just worried about the short-term gains which they can easily attain and earn more money.

The story of corporations is no different. They are busy making products that have less nutritional value but do more harm to people's health. Humans are feeding their children these packaged products which are manufactured in the closed factory set-ups using different forms of preservatives. The products are packaged nicely to make them appear flashy and compelling so that they are really healthy to eat. Then there are added labels that echoes the nutritional value of these products to people's diet. There's hardly any concern in anyone's mind today about the wellbeing of society. Everyone looks busy with just making new products. World is grappling with a lot of problems today and people are continuously engaged in actions that are adding more problems on top of the existing ones. Then with all these created problems, governments, corporations, institutions and closed groups run enormous campaigns stating the purpose and meaning for everyone. The purpose and meaning in solving these problems which in turn would add more problems on top of the existing ones.

There's a story that reflects the after-effects of reactive growth and prosperity without considering its long-term impact and ill-consequences. There was a beautiful kingdom, filled with lush green forests, clean rivers, waterfalls and many other natural resources that made the kingdom rich and prosperous. The king was a very noble, and kind-hearted person. He was always concerned about his people and kingdom. He used to listen to his people very carefully and worked for their betterment and their well-being. His philosophy was that maintaining harmony with nature would lead to abundance, and overall well-being. He was always looking for ways to improve the lives of his people. As he would see any problem cropping up in the kingdom, he would immediately start working towards the solution. Once his advisors came to him with a problem and the problem was not an easy one, it was going to create more issues in the near future. The kingdom's population was growing and the resources in the kingdom would not be sufficient going forward to serve the needs of its people. The resources would be strained and people would suffer in future because of scarcity of resources.

King got concerned on hearing this problem and he asked his advisors to come up with a plan so that they can start addressing this issue immediately to deliver the resolution and save people from any future issues. The advisors came up with a detailed plan of growth. In that plan, they suggested big irrigation projects to increase the agricultural produce and to support this they proposed diversions in the rivers so that the water can be utilized for farming. The plan also contained massive infrastructure developmental projects that included construction of factories to produce goods in a more productive and efficient way. They also suggested expansion of the cities where this whole development would happen. The expanded urban areas would be sufficient to accommodate the growing population and serve the needs of people.

After discussing the plan with his advisors, king believed that this would be in the best interest of his people and kingdom. He approved the plan after detailed discussion and formalization with his advisors. The projects began and, in few years, the whole plan was executed. The whole kingdom underwent a massive transformation and development. But there was a cost to this development and transformation and the cost was the greenery of the kingdom. To accomplish this development project, massive deforestation happened which resulted in clearing of many old forests that were rich in natural resources, nutrients, herbs and much more. Rivers were diverted and the water was routed for irrigation projects. New urban areas now carried new factories and industries that spilled poisonous gases. Initially, it appeared that things have really changed for good. But soon the realization hit the whole kingdom and the king when people started facing the ill-consequences of this growth and transformation.

The rivers that once carried clean water were now filled with polluted waste of industries and factories. The air was polluted and started causing different forms of diseases in people. The fertile soil started losing nutrients and with use of chemical fertilizers, the quality of produce became poor. The forests that once were the source of fresh air and rich in resources and biodiversity were not there to protect the overall climate and shield people from the natural devastation. The people's wellbeing was sacrificed for the sake of this developmental project.

When the kingdom was grappling with the ill-effects of development, a sage visited the kingdom. He has travelled many places and seen effects of similar form of developmental projects. He went to king and warned him that he should stop this destruction immediately, as his reactive and rapid actions of development has created a lot of new problems for the kingdom. The whole issue started with problems that may arise in future. But with this developmental plan execution, the king and his advisors created more problems for people. They played with nature, cleared forests and disrupted the balance of nature that actually provided prosperity and well-being to the kingdom. If this continues, the future generations would hold you responsible for all this destruction and devastation.

The king listened to the sage's words very patiently and understood the grave mistake made by him and his advisors. He looked around and the truth was inevitably clear to him that what he has done to his once beautiful kingdom. His intentions were good, but for short-term correction, his efforts had resulted in the depletion of resources, imbalance in environment and climate, and suffering and diseases among his people. He realized his mistake and learned a lesson that true progress can't be achieved by just addressing the immediate problem at hand, but it requires careful understanding and contemplation of situation and the long-term impact of any planned corrective measures.

The above story of king reflects the actions of the modern humans and society. Today, in the pursuit of solving smaller issues, humans are overlooking the adverse effects of their actions. There's extraction of more resources to feed the factories that's causing elimination of foundational elements of the planet. Deforestation at an alarming rate has disturbed the whole ecological balance and resulted in climate change that's causing more destruction and devastation. Overuse of water from rivers for agriculture and industrial waste being thrown into rivers is making water unfit for drinking and causing diseases among the population. Industrial activity is at its peak and growing across the globe. Industries release harmful pollutants into the air, soil and water. Air pollution from factories and automobiles are causing respiratory problems and climate change. Chemicals used in the agriculture to increase agricultural produce is causing many severe health issues among people. Safe drinking water is becoming unavailable in most urban and rural areas causing severe water scarcity. Over and above this, massive destruction due to floods and increasing sea-water levels is becoming a threat for humans.

Humans are intelligent beings and they think that they can solve any number of problems coming their way. With this notion, many initiatives have been started that are aimed at solving the issues related to environmental changes. But most of the initiatives end up creating more problems in the long run. As an example, dams created as large-scale renewable energy projects, result in disrupting ecosystems and displacement of communities. Large scale highway, railway tracks and other infrastructure projects result in significant deforestation further adding to environmental issues.

There's a saying **"ignorance is bliss"** – it's applicable for situations where the people unaware about the issues don't worry too much about it, but in case of humans in the modern world, ignorance could lead to disaster if accountability and collective responsibility is not taken. Ignoring sustainability would have dire consequences for the entire human race. Humans are already seeing these consequences in form of floods, famine, melting glaciers, rising sea water level and much more. The way humans look at prosperity needs a serious rethinking, as prosperity needs establishing balance with nature and live in harmony with it.

Amazon rainforests often referred to as "Lungs of earth", is threatened with all this deforestation. Deforestation for agriculture, infrastructure, mining etc. has impacted vast areas of the key ecosystem. This has not only impacted the climate, but also threatened countless species living in these forests. All this is contributing to climate change, as all the carbon stored is getting released into the atmosphere. The loss of indigenous communities who have always lived in harmony with nature for generations is also a big threat, as many of these communities have maintained the balance and harmony with nature. The loss of such communities would mean more disaster and destruction going forward.

Many countries have been witnessing the displacement of millions of people because of the rising sea levels. In Bangladesh, flooding situation affected millions of people. Small islands such as Kiribati and Tuvalu are threatened to become unliveable and unhabitable. All these examples across the world highlights the problem at hand and it requires collective and immediate action so that there's a better future for generations to come.

There's need for a robust framework that can support and deliver sustainable future for the generations to come. Humans need to focus on some key areas that might be of help:

- **Sustainability as a practice:** There's need to adopt sustainable practices in each and every walk of life. Right from houses, workplaces to communities, and nations, there's need for collective and collaborative response in form of sustainable practices that can be adopted in the daily lives of people.

E.g., using energy efficient appliances, waste reduction, and supporting local and global sustainable businesses to thrive.

- **Education and awareness about sustainability**: It's important to educate people about the criticality of situation and importance of sustainability. The awareness campaigns, seminars, conferences, communities could be of great value to drive the education and awareness initiatives. Modern era has the biggest tool i.e., technology where social media and other digital media platforms are a good medium to educate people on sustainability initiatives, practices and their role in them.

- **Common policy framework**: There's some serious work that's required on the common and collective policy front. Governments, organizations, institutions need to work together to promote environmental protection and sustainable development. In case of need for changes in the policy framework, immediate intervention and action should be taken to address the change.

- **Support for more sustainable businesses**: Companies and organizations who are working towards the sustainable practices need to be promoted and incentivized to support the long-term impact. People should start choosing products from such companies that prioritize sustainability. Businesses should have equal accountability towards sustainability and environmental impact.

- **More local community support**: Local and global communities should start working towards the common goal of sustainability. At a local level, the communities should enrol more people to support the initiatives that can be replicated across other areas. Similarly, global initiatives need to be run and supported by the communities.

Sustainability is not just a buzz word, it's not something that should be considered as a good to have initiative or even an initiative. It's a way of life and humans need to learn this way of life to make their mark and impact so that future generations can thank them for the collaborative work. Adopting sustainable practices is not just an option, but it's a necessity for the survival of this planet and the future generations. It's important to learn from history, and history has lot of lessons for humans to take motivation. Learning from those past experiences and finding the right guidance is important. By supporting the right initiatives, humans can really drive the real change. The above discussed framework provides a good foundational work that can be done to create a sustainable future. The journey of sustainability is not merely about the show or making a noise, it's about the survival, it's not about profit, it's about our home **"the planet earth"**. The real key to sustainability lies within humans and they need to be making conscious choices, decisions and taking right actions to create a better future for the coming generations.

Let's understand the concept and implications with a short story. Once there lived a wise old woman named Savi, in a small village in middle of a vast dense forest. Savi was known in the village for her ancient knowledge and she was regarded as the protector of nature. Her wisdom was the result of many earlier generations that maintained harmony with nature and preferred living in and with nature. She knew that there's a need to create and maintain balance with nature to sustain life. On a sunny day, a young person named Siva came to Savi. Siva had recently returned from a city where he had studied about the modern technology and innovation, along with business. When he met Savi, he started discussing a lot of transformational ideas for the progress and prosperity of people in the village. He said, we can build factories, harvest the forest's resources and trade them for material wealth and growth. This will really transform the lives of village people and make them prosperous.

Savi was listening to all this patiently. After Siva was finished sharing his idea, Savi said to Siva – "let's go for a walk through the forest". During the walk, Savi talked and pointed towards the long-standing trees, the freely flowing river, the singing birds, and animals of the forest. She said – "Do you realize that this forest is a living being like us, it's fully alive. Every single part of this forest plays an important role in our lives as well. This forest provides us with everything we need for living and surviving on this earth. Be it food, water, air, medicine etc. It has been doing this for generations and will keep on doing this in future as well."

Siva still trying to convince Savi replied – "But there's so much more we can do with all these resources of forest. We can have a great future for our children".

Savi smiled looking towards Siva and pointed towards an old tree, with deep roots and branches flying freely towards the sky. She said, let me tell you a story. Long ago, there was a situation in this village, when villagers were almost on the verge of dying from hunger due to drought. The villagers reacted in hurriedness and they started cutting trees to free up more land for crops. When they were doing this, it appeared as if they are doing a very good thing. The crops were planted and for some time, situation remained pretty good and in control. But later, the soil became barren, the animals started disappearing, rivers dried up. The whole village came closer to destruction.

When all this was happening, an old man came to the village and advised the villagers that forests are not just for exploiting the resources for one's benefit, but they are part of living ecosystem and they have life too. They too need to be well respected and nurtured, as yourself. Villagers heard the old man and realized their mistake. They started planting more trees, worked towards protecting the rivers, and started living in harmony with the nature. With time, the forest came back to life and the whole village prospered as earlier.

After telling this story, Savi took a pause and looked at Siva, "The lesson from this story is that the real prosperity doesn't come from exploitation, but from living in harmony with nature. We get blinded by the material pleasures and wealth, but we must learn to create a balance with nature and not just focus on taking it all from nature, but should become responsible enough to give it back to nature as well".

Siva became silent for a while when he listened to Savi. He was carefully analysing and absorbing what Savi just said. He realized that he had started ignoring the very foundation of their existence, in pursuit of material wealth and pleasure. He understood that the forest was not just a resource to exploit, but a living breathing being that needs to be respected and people should live in harmony with nature.

With this clarity, both started working together for the betterment of villagers. They started educating people about the sustainable practices. They also built small-scale, ecofriendly businesses, that utilized forest resources, but did-not exploit or deplete them. They advised and guided people to plant more trees, clean the rivers, and also focused on living in harmony with nature. The village prospered over time and became a living example of balance, harmony and happiness.

This story of Savi and Siva is a testament that sustainable practices can help attain balance, prosperity, harmony and growth for not only humans but for the entire existence in its entirely. This journey of sustainability is a continuously evolving journey filled with experiences, learnings, struggle and outcomes. At times, it may appear tiring and hectic, but at the end the result is a prosperous and healthy planet with most favourable conditions for the existence. By living sustainably, we not only respect and admire the nature around us, but also create a beautiful environment for the generations to come.

"What do we need is good to ask? But whether it's an absolute necessity for survival, is a more important introspection to happen. And then it should be followed by another intriguing and corrective ask that how much do we need?" When all this inherent curiosity is put in consensus then it's easier and worthwhile to arrive at the outcomes. The traditional societies that thrived for so long have continuously focused on asking these right questions at all times. They use to come and sit together, discuss and sense what's the utmost important and urgent tasks to accomplish, accordingly the decisions were being taken. These societies thrived in harmony with nature for centuries just because they followed a set of identified and established practices that helped them achieve this. They understood the need to preserve the national environment, recognize the importance of their decisions and their long-term impact on the overall ecosystem. The collective wisdom and consensus between people helped these societies thrive and prepare a better future for their coming generations as well. Modern humans need to rethink their priorities and look around to sense the urgency of sustainable practices that must be established and followed with rigor to create a better future for their coming generations.

The technological innovation achieved so far should be used and pivoted to support the sustainability work and approach. Humans can utilize the advancements in data analysis and environmental science to gain understanding of the resources and their level of usage. When humans learn to utilize technology for the benefit of everyone by just creating enough that's required to meet the needs, then a sustainable future is not a distant dream to achieve. Mindfulness and conscious decision making are equally important to achieve this dream.

Sustainability is a shared responsibility where governments, communities, institutions, closed groups have to come together to work towards a better future. The actions need to be decided in consensus and the new practices established should be passed on as a framework to the coming generations so that they can continue working towards the common goal of sustainability and provide the same gift to their next generations.

The relentless chase for wealth and power led to the fall,

Nature's treasure depleting, none's listening to the nature's cry and call,

The illusion and lust for more and more, an unending blinded quest,

Once the time and resources run out of hand, there won't be any moment left to rest.

Forests destroyed for fortune, rivers getting poisonous and running dry,

Minerals sucked from mountains, under a polluted sky,

The environment once pure and clean, now filled with toxic haze,

A living example of human greed, in such dark and troubled days.

Climate change is the result of this endless reckless need,

A burning planet, rising oceans, fertile land now filled with weed,

Unbounded desires unchecked by voice of wisdom,

Ceaseless flood of human wants, left little to no thinking room seldom.

Lost biodiversity, many species eliminated in silent scream,

Once rich planet, now lost and have become a distant dream,

Drained of natural resources, planet's veins running dry,

No more healthy environments, under the hazy and polluted sky.

Humans have turned a deaf ear to nature's cry and pushing
forward in plight,

Behind the wealth and possessions, completely blind to the nature's right,

Many claims on sustainability, but efforts are half-hearted and weak,

Excuses spoken with hollow words; actions hardly ever speak.

There's a mad, destructive race, being run by everyone,

Very few pause to think and consider, but the fragility considered by none,

Continuing on this path, with unchecked and ignored wisdom,

Destruction awaits all, the dire tragedy hovering over the earthly kingdom.

It's high time to cease the endless race, and adopt a different way,

That allows to live in harmony with earth, each and every single day,

It's not the wealth, possessions or power that will last and be passed on,

It's the ultimate harmony and care of each-other and nature that will l
ead the way.

Chapter 11

THE SALT OF SPIRITUALITY – "IS IT A HIDDEN TREASURE AND BLESSING FOR THE MODERN TIMES?"

—————————❧❧—————————

"The dialogue between Ashtavakra and King Janaka" – *"You are born free and can remain free if you understand that anything and everything is just an illusion and attachment. Being an observer is the very first step towards achieving the real freedom, the freedom that's eternal, the freedom that's the nature of being, of the atman (the soul)"*

When Ashtavakra *(a great saint and master of ancient times)* was young. He accompanied his father to the great spiritual debate that used to happen in King Janaka's court. King Janaka was a keen seeker and was curious to understand the way to enlightenment. He used to finish his duties at the earliest possible and spare his time so that he can spend it in the court hearing to all these spiritual debates between the learned sages and one of his most learned and wise ministers. On one occasion, Ashtavakra's father engaged in a debate with one of king's most learned ministers. Ashtavakra was not there with his father on that day. The debate progressed and his father started losing the debate. When Ashtavakra got to know about it, he headed to the court. But he was stopped at the gate by the soldier and the soldier laughed at his appearance, as his all eight limbs were deformed. After much request and by taking permission from the King Janaka, Ashtavakra was allowed into the court. As he entered the court, all the ministers and the whole so called learned group started laughing at him. Ashtavakra looked at Janka at said **"Is one's body the sole projection of his/her wisdom?"**. It appears that this court is just worried about physical appearance and not curious about the real wisdom as perceived outside this court.

King Janaka and everyone else suddenly became silent after listening to Ashtavakra. King Janaka felt a sense of guilt after hearing to Ashtavakra that he too laughed at his deformities like everyone else. After this the story is around Janaka's seeking of truth and Ashtavakra's discourse that helped Janaka quench his thirst of seeking enlightenment. The dialogue between the two is an in-depth exploration of true nature of self and the reality of existence. The learnings gained through this dialogue with Ashtavakra helped Janaka get free from the entanglements of this material world and material possessions and move beyond the body to experience real self. The real self is beyond the body and to get beyond the body one needs to be a keen observer and understand the difference between the doer and observer. One should be able to understand that he/she is just an observer and the observation brings in the profound realization about self and the atman *(soul)* which is the essence of existence. As Janaka learned that the true self, is like the salt in the ocean and is always present. Humans should imbibe this learning as the foundation of existence, as it can create phenomenal difference in ways of creating and maintaining life on this planet. This would help with dissolution of ego, desires and attachments so that one can taste the real flavour of existence through spirituality. Ashtavakra's story and the learnings share the great truth that following the path of spirituality can lead one to the real and true understanding of self that can further help to make this world a better place to live.

"The spiritual philosophy of middle path – Gautam Buddha" *– "One needs to achieve balance in life, as letting go is the first step towards realization. Desires and attachments are the roots of suffering, so one needs to be careful with them. Avoiding extremities and trying to find balance, is the way towards leading a spiritual, realized life that's free from distortions of desires and attachments"*

When Siddhartha Gautam realized that human life is not at all about just happiness and prosperity and this body suffers from all kinds of ailments and loose strength with aging; mind suffers from stress and anxiety that are result of all attachments and desires, he left for an unknown search and exploration for the real purpose and truth of human existence. After spending many years in struggle with an unwavering focus towards achieving the ultimate truth and wisdom, he experienced realization while resting under the Bodhi tree. After realization, he went on to share his experiences in form of teachings with his friends and disciples. He was later called as **Budha, which means "the one who has achieved and attained enlightenment and who is free from all desires and attachments of this material world"**. During his journey of exploration, Budha realized that one needs to become an observer and just let go off all the distractions of this world as they arise such as desires, fears, illusions, attachments. It's a difficult task to become an observer, as human tendency is to get involved in all the thoughts, desires and attachments and consider self as the one who is solely responsible for everything. Budha's teachings to the world states, **"to experience the ultimate truth one needs to be free from attachments, as attachments bring suffering and once humans learn to just let go, they would be free from all the suffering humanity is facing."**

Teachings of Buddha says that awareness is the key to dissolution of the bonds of suffering. Awareness is just like the salt that dissolves into water, it dissolves all the human desires as they come, leaving behind just **"the true self"**. In no way, these teachings tell us to run away from the obstacles and challenges of life, but instead they teach us to see them with clarity without getting attached with them and find liberation. Life of Buddha was about finding balance, as he moved from extreme luxury of being a prince to the harsh life of a monk. While in both these extremities, he was away from finding balance and thus the realization. But when he abandoned both, he found enlightenment on the middle path. This middle path is the essence of Buddha's teachings, which clearly reflects that the true realization happens when there's balance. Balance is the salt of life, that avoids the extremes and help humans live the life of balance and realization.

This middle path is like a radar of ship which keeps on guiding humans in each and every aspect of life. One should learn to attain balance in all aspects of life whether it's material, spiritual or emotional. Once humans learn to live in balance, they would be able to live a life which is spiritual, grounded in truth and free from all extremities.

"The path of Ahimsa (non-violence), truth and Aparigraha (non-possession) – Mahavira" – *"One needs to practice discipline and commitment to adhere to the foundations of truth, non-violence, non-stealing, chastity and non-possession to gain progress on the spiritual path."*

Vardhamana was born into a royal family and from a very young age he was inclined towards the spiritual path. In his early 30's, he renounced everything to pursue the path of truth and realization. He struggled for 12 years wandering, practicing severe penance, and meditation. He was focused on achieving purification of mind and soul through these practices and he continued on the path till he attained the ultimate wisdom, Kevala Jnana (omniscience). His path reflects the need for purification of self and freedom from all worldly entanglements and possessions to attain liberation. He is known for his teachings on Ahimsa (non-violence), as per which every being on this planet has a soul that deserves respect and compassion. His teachings clearly reflected in his whole life, words and actions. His idea of Ahimsa is the very foundation of achieving spiritual growth, as any form of violence hinders spiritual growth of humans.

There are five foundations/pillars of Jainism called as the **five vows.** Mahavira established the five vows as – Satya (truth), Ahimsa (non-violence), Asteya (non-stealing), Brahmacharya (chastity), and Aparigraha (non-possession). These five principles form the foundation of spiritual practice and those following them would find progress in the spiritual path leading to liberation. These foundations help seekers preserve and purify their soul through discipline and commitment, thus preventing any form of corruption that can deviate the seeker from the spiritual path and progress. They help seekers to save themselves from the corrupting influences of worldly pleasures and attachments.

All these teachings whether of Buddha, Mahavira or Ashtavakra have the same message – **"Life is about internal well-being, purification, and freedom, rather than focusing on external illusion that's just a distraction in the path of attaining and living the true meaning of life"**. Throughout the journey of evolution, humans have undergone huge transformation in their thinking, acting, behaving and creating things. Sometimes they got carried away with their sense of security and comfort, that led to the creation of this whole artificial world that we see around us today. At other times, they led internal exploration to search for the true freedom and that resulted in many philosophies that projected a path of living with freedom and compassion. All the teachings discussed above have one thing in common and that's **"the need for real freedom"**. Humans have this unending thirst for freedom from the very beginning. They have been searching for attaining true freedom and in that search, they have created so many different religions, philosophies and principles. All these philosophies focus on creating a practice, a path that can lead humans towards the freedom. Most of these spiritual practices and philosophies talk about going beyond the body and that's possible for human beings as they have this ability with all these emotions and intelligence that can lead the way for them.

Going beyond the body is not an external effort, it's an internal introspection and path of realization. One need to become a keen observer and start observing the thoughts as they arise. When the thoughts give rise to desires, one need to observe that transition carefully so that they are aware of the source of the desire. Once the root of desire is known and carefully watched, then at that very moment the realization can happen through observation. True realization can happen when humans start watching their actions carefully, as that's the place to start with. It's very difficult for someone to start with thoughts, as thoughts are not easy to watch, capture, observe and identify. Thoughts arise in human mind as the currents in the sea, it's very difficult to distinguish them. So, it's easier to start with what's easy to observe and comprehend and that's human action. One should carefully watch his/her actions and practice moving backwards from there. Most spiritual practices teach that one should sit silently at one place to observe thoughts and desires. But for someone who is just starting, it's important to start with observation of his/her daily life.

Start with observing your actions on a daily basis. Once you start observing yourself daily, you will start realizing that there are many actions that need correction and amendment. There are many reactions that shouldn't have happened in the first place. There are many thoughts that shouldn't have come to your mind. But it would be difficult to distinguish all this in the beginning. But once you start doing this and continue for some time, you will realize that some corrections have already started and you have automatically corrected some of your actions, reactions and thoughts. Once this is achieved, then the next step is to move backwards, start observing your thoughts carefully and for this you might need to spare sometime when you can sit silently and just watch your thoughts as they come and go. Practicing this for few days will help you reach a state where you'll be carefully watching your thoughts and will be able to distinguish between them as well.

The progress on the spiritual path is gradual but fulfilling. Humans are born to live a meaningful life and spirituality provides that meaning to human life. Spirituality is not a discovery, but it's a way of life that needs to be followed by humans. Humans have the ability to act, transform, change their surroundings. They have this ability to care and be compassionate about the surroundings including the environment, its elements, and other living beings. Early human beings used to live in harmony with nature and care about other beings as well. Their way of life was spiritual in essence. But today as humans have progressed so much, they have somehow lost that connection with nature and other fellow beings. Their path is completely different and diverted. The spiritual path is completely lost and the progress is being made on the material path, the path of making. Human mind is crowded with the relentless pursuit of material possessions, and there's no space left for the spiritual progress which is the real way of life.

In essence, it's obvious **"why humans have become so vulnerable today?"**. Look around and see people struggling in their lives just because they are leading a very unconscious life. They are motivated with false sense of achieving more material possessions, as that's what have become the criteria of success in today's world. Human confidence is just like a filled air bubble, which can easily burst on slightest disturbance in the surrounding environment. Humans have lost control of their lives just because they have become slaves to their emotions, desires and pursuit of more and more. There's need to get back to the old wisdom that can help get back the control of life. Consciousness is the key to live peacefully and freely. Modern humans need to work backwards to gain back their consciousness and become more aware about their environment, surroundings, nature and their whole self. There should be focus on the key pillars of life which includes – truth, peace, care, compassion and realization.

The path to realization is not an easier one, but it's not a difficult one either. What's needed is just the awakening and conscious effort to walk towards the destination. Humans need to understand that life is about deep connection with the environment and nature. The survival is not about domination, but it's about staying in harmony with nature. There's need to be thankful about the environment, the skies, the seas, forests and other beings as well. This change can really create a beautiful future for humans and their coming generations. The sense of interconnectedness should become a way of life, deeply embedded in the daily practices.

Today whole humanity is at crossroads, with relentless pursuit of material possessions, wealth, power and progress bringing the whole environment at the verge of collapse and there's deep discontentment everywhere. The life of modern humans filled with constant rush, ceaseless demands have completely overshadowed the peaceful and steady voice of spirituality. Humans have moved forward, away from the peacefulness and freedom, but there's still hope to turn back and see inside, where lies the potential to rediscover the peace and freedom that's much needed. There's desperate need to realign the way of life with principles of conscious living. Conscious living requires awareness about the present moment, to act with intention, and to learn and acknowledge the impact of our actions on our lives. Such living requires turning back to simplicity, with no measuring scale for success based on accumulations and control.

The answers to meaning and purpose are hidden in the spirituality. This has been with humans since beginning, in form of the wisdom passed on by early humans, but it somehow faded away with greed, selfishness and corruption that clouded the human mind. Prioritizing the spiritual growth over material growth is the prime need of today's society, as humans need to learn compassion over competition, cooperation over conflict and sustainability over exploitation and unending material progress. Spirituality enhances the quality and flavour of life and existence. It adds depth and meaning to our thoughts and actions. Without spirituality life becomes directionless and meaningless, which results in discontentment and disaster.

As we move towards the closer of this journey of understanding, let's take with us some important learnings, especially the learning of spirituality which is going to be the revival antidote for the modern world and generations to come. Spirituality is not a destination, but it's a journey that needs to be covered by each and every generation. The methods might be different, but the path and essence would remain the same. We need to be careful with the choices we make today, as that's going to define and decide our future along with the future of coming generations. Let's carry this compass of spirituality with us, so that it can become a guide for us to navigate through the challenges coming our way. Let's come together to learn and live consciously, to live in harmony with our environment and nature, as our ancestors did. Let's not put a blind eye to the devastation caused around through our actions, and collectively work towards making things better for coming generations.

Remember, "**the greatest gift one can leave behind is the real wisdom that can continue to guide generations to come on the righteous path, the path of harmony, truth, compassion, and the path of ultimate realization**".

In the chase for more material wealth, we lost our way,

Left behind the light of wisdom that guided our way,

We raced to the sky with all our might,

Missed the heavenly guide, that taught us to think and behave right.

The real essence and salt of life, is in realization and wisdom,

Not in the riches or land or any earthly or heavenly kingdom,

Our duty is to listen to the internal call,

However quiet, still or small.

We won the world, but lost the heart,

Broken in fragments, we fell and torn apart,

Deep inside, there are whispers of an ancient cry,

A simple truth is told again, leaving it on us to follow and try.

The heavenly path to peace was and is not in the gain,

But in the real love, caring and compassion that heals the pain,

Living in tune with nature and surroundings is the way it should be,

That's the path for body and soul to be entirely free.

Oh dear, so take a deep breath and look within,

The journey doesn't end but begins here,

On the path of spirituality, that's pure and right,

Revealing the true meaning, where we find the light!

www.ingramcontent.com/pod-product-compliance
Lightning Source LLC
Chambersburg PA
CBHW042047150726
48005CB00034B/2202